CHICKEN SOUP
FOR THE
CHRISTIAN
TEENAGE SOUL

Chicken Soup for the Christian Teenage Soul
Stories of Faith, Love, Inspiration and Hope
Jack Canfield, Mark Victor Hansen, Kimberly Kirberger, Patty Aubery,
Nancy Mitchell-Autio

Published by Backlist, LLC,
a unit of Chicken Soup for the Soul Publishing, LLC. www.chickensoup.com

Front cover design by Larissa Hise Henoch
Originally published in 2003 by Health Communications, Inc.

Back cover and spine redesign by Pneuma Books, LLC

Distributed to the booktrade by Simon & Schuster. SAN: 200-2442

Publisher's Cataloging-in-Publication Data
(Prepared by The Donohue Group)

Chicken soup for the Christian teenage soul : stories of faith, love, inspiration
and hope / [compiled by] Jack Canfield ... [et al.].

p. : ill. ; cm.

Originally published: Deerfield Beach, FL : Health Communications, c2003.
ISBN: 978-1-62361-010-4

1. Christian teenagers--Religious life--Anecdotes. 2. Anecdotes. I. Canfield,
Jack, 1944-

BV4531.3 .C485 2012
242/.63   2012944062

PRINTED IN THE UNITED STATES OF AMERICA
on acid free paper

21 20 19 18 17 16 15 14 13 12   01 02 03 04 05 06 07 08 09 10

CHICKEN SOUP
FOR THE
CHRISTIAN
TEENAGE SOUL

Stories of Faith, Love, Inspiration and Hope

Jack Canfield
Mark Victor Hansen
Kimberly Kirberger
Patty Aubery
Nancy Mitchell-Autio

Backlist, LLC, a unit of
Chicken Soup for the Soul Publishing, LLC
Cos Cob, CT
www.chickensoup.com

Dear God,
Please receive our heartfelt gratitude and thanks
for all teenagers. Please bless them and help them
see their path to You. We pray for their happiness, their
growth and their good. May their lives be
illuminated by Your light. May they find that for
which they are seeking. And may their hearts be
filled with Your love.

Amen.

Contents

10. THY WILL BE DONE

Introduction

Dear Teens,

We have come a long way together. Since the first
Chicken Soup for the Teenage Soul book came out in 1997, we
have heard from hundreds of thousands of you. You have
written letters, and you have e-mailed. You have called,
and you have posted messages in our Web site forums.
You have shared with us, and you have confided in us.

As a result, we know that your connection and relationship with God are important to you. We have been
deeply moved by the expressions of faith in the letters
and stories you send. Many of you have requested a
Chicken Soup book especially for Christian teenagers, so
we have written and compiled this book for you.

We hope you find that the stories in this book reflect
your spiritual experiences—your devotion, your lessons,
your longings and your beliefs. The teenagers in this book
write about love, compassion, loss, forgiveness, gratitude
and blessings. They offer their personal experiences to
uplift your spirits, inspire your faith and encourage your
relationship with God.

This book is for those hoping to deepen and strengthen
their faith in God. It will also provide solace and comfort
for those questioning their relationship with God. Finally,

it is a powerful introduction to what it means to be a Christian teen for those curious about Christianity or exploring Christianity for the first time.

May this book inspire and deepen your relationship with God, and may you always be blessed by God's grace.

All our love,
Kimberly, Jack, Mark, Patty and Nancy

1

ON FAITH

Faith is the substance of things hoped for, the evidence of things not seen.

Hebrews 11:1

Sometimes

Sometimes I question you,
And wonder whether you're listening.
I can't see you, or touch you, or even feel you,
So how do I know if you're really there?

Sometimes I get mad at you,
When I see bad things happen to good people.
I wonder why you wouldn't save them.
It makes me wonder if you're real.

Sometimes when I pray to you,
I can sense that you are there with me,
Watching over me as your child,
Blessing me with your grace.

Sometimes when I can see you clearly,
When I see little babies or kind smiles,
Generous people and the beauty of nature,
It makes me believe with my whole heart.

Sometimes my questions about you don't matter,
Even though there are never definite answers.
I have faith in your love.
Forgive me, God, for ever questioning you.

Jenny Sharaf

Rescue Me

More tears are shed over answered prayers than unanswered ones.

Mother Teresa

My high school was in a border town, meaning we got new students who came over with their families from Mexico. Sometimes they'd speak English, and sometimes they didn't. We wouldn't normally mingle with these kids. We just sort of stuck with our own group.

Leticia was different. She was one of those girls who walks in a room, and everything gets all fuzzy and slow motion, like in the movies. She had long, dark hair and the greenest eyes I'd ever seen. She smiled as she walked by, and even though it probably wasn't at me, I took it as a sign.

I'm not usually the "lucky" type, but fate seemed to be smiling down on me because it turned out she was in most of my classes. The first time she was called on in U.S. History, she knew the answer (which I didn't), and she spoke in perfect English. I later found out she was from Mexico City and had studied American History at her school there. This totally intimidated me.

On April 11, I was sitting in U.S. History, totally stressing about a midterm we were having the next day. I didn't even notice the guidance counselor come in to talk to our teacher, Mr. Huston. When he called my name, I didn't hear him. Then I looked up, and both he and the counselor had strange expressions on their faces, and they were looking at me. Something was wrong. I figured I was in trouble, but I couldn't imagine for what.

I followed the guidance counselor down the hall and into her office. When we got there, the principal was there, too. They were both silent for a minute. Then the principal began to speak.

"Your father has had a heart attack. The paramedics and doctors did everything they could to save him, but I'm afraid he didn't make it."

"Okay," I said. "Well, I'd better be getting back to class. I don't want to miss the rest of the exam review."

They looked at me, stunned. I didn't really know what I was saying. I felt like they were telling me about someone else's dad. I just didn't get it.

The next few weeks were a blur as we had the funeral and began adjusting to life without my dad. I went back to school after I ran out of things to do at home. Everything felt a little different. I can't exactly explain how; it just did.

Back at school everyone was super-nice to me. The teachers didn't call on me, and they kept asking me to stay after class to see if I was "okay." My friends were really weird. I felt like I couldn't talk to them about the same old things. It was all so strange. My dad was a great guy, and then all of a sudden he was dead. He didn't do anything wrong. He never hurt anyone. I started eating lunch alone. I just couldn't deal with listening to the same stupid jokes or talking about random stuff.

About three weeks after I went back to school, I was sitting in a corner of the quad, not really eating, just staring off into space. "Are you going to eat the rest of that sandwich?" I looked up and saw Leticia standing in front of me.

"Huh?" I responded. I looked down and realized I hadn't touched my sandwich. I handed it over.

As she gratefully accepted, she told me, "My mom packed me a meat and egg torta. Your tuna fish looks better." She sat down next to me and ate my sandwich. She didn't say a word to me, but seemed happy to just sit there.

After a few minutes, I grew too uncomfortable. "Why did you come over?" I asked.

"You looked like you could use a friend," she said. "I lost my father last year." I didn't know what to say to her, and she didn't know what to say to me. I didn't want to talk about my dad, but for the first time in a while, I felt okay just being with another person.

We started having lunch together on that bench every day. We never mentioned my dad or her dad, except she told me that was the reason they moved from Mexico. We talked about school, TV and movies and other meaningless stuff. I loved her mom's tortas, and she seemed to like my "American" sandwiches. I finally worked up the nerve to ask her to go to a movie with me.

"I'd like to," she said, "but I have to ask you a question first. Are you a Christian?"

"Huh?" I replied.

She told me her dad was a deeply spiritual man, and that it had been very important to him that she associate only with Christians. Basically, she was saying she couldn't go out with me unless I believed in the same stuff she did. I was confused. She had become my friend, and up till now she didn't care if I was a Christian or not.

I told her I wanted to go out with her, but I didn't think I was a Christian *and* I didn't think it should matter. Unfortunately, I then said something really stupid. I said, "It doesn't matter to me that you're Mexican." She looked at me, then got up and walked away.

A week went by. I came to the bench every day with a tuna-fish sandwich in hopes Leticia would show up. No luck. But finally one day she was there.

"To love the Lord with all your heart, mind, soul and strength, and your neighbor as yourself, means to experience forgiveness and to forgive others as well as yourself. Matthew 6:12." That's all she said. Then she took my tuna sandwich and started eating it.

So we went back to our routine of daily lunch and sandwich exchange. I didn't bring up the dating thing again, and neither did she. The prom was coming up, and I really wanted to ask her.

"So what does it take to become a Christian, anyway? Do I have to shave my head or go spend the night in the woods or something?"

She ignored my sarcasm. "No, all you have to do is pray with me."

"All I have to do is pray?" That seemed pretty easy.

"Well, there is one catch," she said. "You have to mean it. I mean, *really* mean it. You have to give up your soul to God. You have to beg forgiveness for all your sins. Can you do that?"

Sure, I thought. *A little prayer and I get to take Leticia to the prom.* "Okay," I said. "Let's do it. Where do we go?"

"How about right here?" she responded.

"In front of everyone?"

"Why not?" She told me to close my eyes. Then she started to pray. She asked me to invite God's spirit into my heart. I started to say the words after her and stopped. I saw this image in my mind of a closed door. I was about to open it and go through. I could see light streaming through the keyhole. We were silent for a long time as I had my hand on the doorknob. Then I turned it and opened the door.

I started to cry. I cried for my father. I cried for my mother and sister. I cried for Leticia's father. I cried for all the kids who lost their fathers and mothers. I couldn't stop crying. I felt God's grace.

Leticia and I went to the prom, and we had a great time. We're seniors now, and we're still together. I miss my dad a lot, and I think about him all the time. I still don't have all the answers. But I owe Leticia a lot because she gave me my faith. She rescued me.

Matt Rivers

"We especially like your sermons on your Web site because we can scroll through them quickly."

Reprinted by permission of Harley Schwadron.

Our Day to Give Thanks

*True thanksgiving means that we need to thank
God for what he has done for us and not to tell
him what we have done for him.*

George R. Hendrick

I remember when I was a boy growing up in Texas. My
dad would always say that each Sunday was our day to
give thanks. I never understood what he meant by this,
but each Sunday we would go to church and pray to God
and Jesus Christ. As I recall, I didn't like going because my
friends would be playing football or baseball while I
would be inside studying the Bible.

My dad worked construction and was a very private
man who never said much. For as long as I can remember,
it was always just him and me. I never really knew my
mom, but my dad said that after I was born she had fallen
in love with another man. He never liked to talk about her,
and I never really liked to talk about how much I missed
her. I would think of her mostly on Sundays when he and
I were at church. I would always ask God why he took my

mom away, but no matter how much I prayed he never answered. Sometimes I could tell my dad was asking God the same thing.

As I got older, we would still keep the same routine: church every Sunday and the occasional baseball game afterwards. I liked the game, and although my dad never really cared for it, he would still take me after services. I think it was his way of staying even, since he knew I didn't like going to church that much. When I was a freshman in high school, he even agreed to let me try out for the baseball team at school. When I told him I had made it, I could tell he was really proud, even though he didn't say much. Although he was always strict on his rules, my dad and I couldn't have gotten along without one another. All in all, my dad and I were happy.

I think it was October when the principal at my school interrupted class and asked me to come to her office. I was afraid of what she was going to say, and when I got there she said my dad had gotten in a bad accident at work. My eyes began to fill with tears, but I held them back, knowing he would want me to be strong.

When I got to the hospital, the doctors said he was in intensive care and that I couldn't see him. Never in my life had I been so scared, and never in my life did I need God more than at that moment. I sat in that waiting room for what seemed like forever until finally my dad's friend came and picked me up. He told me that a truck's gates holding steel beams had come unlocked and pinned my dad underneath them. When I heard this, I instantly thought of God—not in prayer but in anger—an anger I had never felt in my life. I had always deep down blamed God for taking away my mom, and all of a sudden it seemed he was going take my dad, too.

The next day they said I could visit him, but only for a short time. He looked so bad I wanted to cry, but I saw his face brighten when I entered the room, so I couldn't.

His voice was raspy, and all he told me was to pray for him. That Sunday I went to church alone. Once there, all I could do was look at the empty seat my dad usually filled. I cried as I did what he had asked me to do—pray.

As I prayed, I told Jesus how much I loved him and my dad. Later that day, I got a call saying that my dad's situation had improved, and within a month he would be back home with me again.

After he returned, we decided to move to Colorado where his brother and his wife lived so they could take care of him for a while. Although he still wasn't 100 percent well, he was alive, and I was very happy about that. I told him that I prayed for him just like he asked me to, and he said, "I know you did, son."

Now when Dad says that Sundays are our days to give thanks, I know what he means. I think of God and Jesus Christ, and I give thanks for all they have given us.

Michael Manzi

Searching and Finding

And ye shall seek me and find me when ye shall search for me with all your heart.

Jeremiah 29:13

I am a reader, and readers are dreamers and searchers. All readers, like me, know in their hearts that there is more to life than what they are living. Somewhere, there must be a handsome prince, a dashing rogue, a rugged mountain man to sweep me off my feet and bear me to a land bursting with myth and legend and beautiful scenery. And in that land I would uncover mysteries and secrets, things so simple and pure they can only be found in nature. I would breathe in the fresh, clean air and drink the sounds of birds and breezes and brooks, the soft, supple sounds. There I would be fulfilled and happy. At peace, at last.

For me this dreamland was Ireland. I was ushered to this place through my imagination and by the poetry of William Butler Yeats, especially his description of "The Lake Isle of Innisfree." He painted a picture of peace that he longed for and could only find on that island. He pined after it so, that no matter where he was he would "hear it in the deep heart's core." In my deep heart's core I felt exactly that longing, that need for more; I was drawn to this place of peace.

Until recently, I thought that my vision of Ireland must remain simply a vision. But through the kindness of my grandparents, I was able to go. And, oh the excitement and joy that was mine. I journeyed there with all my hopes and dreams prepared to be fulfilled. And I saw the castles and the bogs, the mountains, the fairy forts, flowers and even the Isle of Innisfree. The beauty was indescribable. The hundreds of radiant flowers pleased my eyes. The sweet sounds of the birds and brooks and breezes soothed my ears. The fragrance of the pure air invigorated my nostrils. I could taste the rain and feel the serenity drop onto my skin and cleanse my soul. But the one sense that remained untouched was my heart. I was still searching, and for days I pulled at the land, needing that fulfillment I thought it offered. But I couldn't find it, and still I felt sad and empty.

One day I was looking deep into a blossom at its incredible beauty and worth, and I remembered how that flower first appeared. The source of its life, the source of mine, the very beginning, the light of life was where and only where I could find my fulfillment and peace of mind. And then my heart exploded, full of what was there all the time, what I could only find within myself, what so many people need and search for, but don't see because it is so simple and basic. And God is basic. God is the source of all things. God is our roots, and just as a tree looks to its roots for nourishment and a river looks to its source for replenishing waters, we must look to our roots and our source to fill the void in our hearts. God is our only nourishment; all else is transient.

So now I read, but I search no longer, because all the romance and adventure enticing me into the worlds between the pages is just a faint taste of the adventure of life, of my life. I am excited about each day as it comes; each one can be made to be fulfilling in its own right. And when my days run out, I will have lived just a blink of time and the rest will be eternal joy. And that is what I learned in Ireland.

Abby Danielle Burlbaugh

Louisa's Bouquet

*In life, as in football, you won't go far unless
you know where the goalposts are.*

Arnold H. Glasgow

Most of us would find it easy to name all our emotional
tugs to the word "friend." We'd say they stick with us
through thick and thin, become bridges over troubled
water, share our secrets, forgive our follies and applaud
our successes.

Then there are the people who peek into our lives,
rearrange us and slip away before we even know they
were our friends.

Such was Louisa.

Louisa and I were not the two most visible people in our
large high school. In fact, if you had asked our classmates
to describe us in one word, most of them would have chosen, "Who?" We met in gym class and became talk-and-
walk-out-to-the-soccer-field companions. She talked
about her plans and goals for a better life and everything
she thought God had called her to be. No more traveling

to work the harvest—she wanted to be the first in her family to go to college. She would provide a better life for her dad and mom and help her brothers and sister through school. She would live a faith-filled life and in the end go to eternity with God.

She worked toward her future in the decisions she made each day. She worked hard for good grades, took speech class for confidence, took an etiquette class for style and worked after school to save all she could for college after pitching in to help her family. When I shared my plans, she would never let me just dream away to someday. She would ask me the who, what, where, when and why questions to help me define and refine my goals until she was satisfied that my plan was worked all the way through. She'd say, "Listen to God, do all you can do and leave the rest to Him."

Our relationship came to an abrupt end three weeks later. On Friday we walked out to the soccer field, and the next Monday we didn't.

And we never did again. Louisa died. She came down with meningitis and died. Just like that.

I couldn't wrap myself around the reality of her death. Louisa had helped me to see my possibilities, to be honest about my strengths and just as honest about my weaknesses. To see the building of long-term dreams in the day-to-day decisions, then to bunch them all together and present them to God with as much joy and innocence as a child giving her mother a bouquet of wildflowers and weeds.

But I was still walking out to the soccer field, and Louisa was gone. For the next few weeks I played while Louisa was heavy in my heart—until the day she shouted the answer to me. At least, I like to believe it was her.

I was running down the field in control of the soccer ball. "Go for the goal, Louisa!" the team captain yelled. The mistake in our names breezed through my head.

I always passed the ball, not because I was a team player, but because I was fully confident in my inability to score a point. "Louisa, go for the goal!" the captain yelled again. I saw the net, I knew what steps to take, I took my shot, and the ball smashed in.

"You did it, Louisa! You made it," the team chorused. My sorrow began to be replaced with understanding.

"You did it, Louisa," I whispered to my faraway friend.

And she had. Louisa had reached her highest goal first. She had lived her life with faith and hope, and she was now with God.

"You made it," I said through my tears.

When your somedays have come and gone, you may look back and be surprised to find that your best friends were not always the funniest ones, the smartest ones or the ones you've kept since kindergarten. You may just find that your truest friend was the one who tiptoed into your life, taught you to pick your bouquet and then quietly slipped away.

Cynthia M. Hamond

"Remember, son, winning isn't everything.
You need good endorsement deals, too."

Winning the Race

I sat in the doctor's office, cradling my pounding head in my hands. Piercing headaches had been hammering me for days, and I prayed that the doctor would be able to find the cause.

"These stupid headaches had better go away by Saturday," I told my mom. "I have to race in the regional meet. The team's counting on me."

"I know, honey," she replied softly. "Let's see what the doctor says."

I was irritated by Mom's casual response. These were the regional cross-country championships! Even though I was only a college freshman, I'd had a great season, and I wanted to keep it going—for me and for my team. I sighed and began massaging my aching temples. I looked up when the door opened, and the doctor stepped inside.

"We've determined what's causing your headaches," he said. He hesitated, then continued, "You've got a tumor in the parietal and occipital lobes of your brain."

My stomach dropped. *What? A brain tumor? Me? No way!* I was a healthy all-American runner who had just led her team to a conference championship. I'd never had any serious health problem. Sure, I'd been having headaches, nausea and dizziness for a few days, but I thought it was just a horrible flu or something. But a *brain tumor?*

Mom didn't accept it, either. "No!" she insisted. "Johanna's *eighteen years old.* That must be wrong."

"I wish it were," the doctor said. "It's not a huge mass— it's about the size of your thumb. But we must remove it immediately to find out if it's cancerous."

As if that news weren't bad enough, there was more. "This is not an aggressive tumor," the doctor said, "but there's a slim chance it could grow back."

I didn't know what to say or think. My head continued to pound as my mind went numb.

"I know this is a lot to take in," the doctor said, "but I'd like to discuss the next steps. . . . "

His words seemed muffled, distant, like when you're waking up from a dream. But this was no dream. This was my harsh reality. And no matter how fast I ran, I couldn't run away from this.

Running Is Life: The Rest Is Just Details. That's what my favorite T-shirt says. And ever since I ran my first race as a second grader, that's how I've felt. While my friends were jumping rope and playing kickball, I was running.

By the time I reached high school, running was my passion. God blessed me with the gift of speed, and I thrived in a competitive atmosphere. I always believed I could win, and that attitude helped me win five cross-country conference championships in high school.

My success continued during the fall cross-country season my freshman year at college. But the shocking news of my brain tumor made me wonder if I'd tasted my last victory.

On the ride home from the doctor's office, I looked down at my jittery hands. They hadn't stopped shaking since I had heard the diagnosis.

After Mom pulled in the driveway and shut off the car, I just sat there, paralyzed by shock ... fear ... dread. Mom reached over, cradling me in her arms. I slouched down and laid my throbbing head in her lap. I couldn't handle these splitting headaches much longer. My operation was in three days. *Will it work?* I wondered. *Will my headaches stop?* I needed relief.

And I needed to process this horrific news, but I didn't know how. Competitive athletics had taught me to tackle any challenge head-on, no matter how difficult. But this challenge was unlike any I'd ever faced. Although I wanted to be positive, I was worried how this tumor would affect me—and my running. After all, running defined me. I couldn't imagine living if I couldn't run. I wanted to know, *After surgery, how long 'til I can run again?*

I didn't have to wait long to start getting some answers. The surgery went well and brought great news: The tumor wasn't cancerous! But since I'm so competitive, I didn't celebrate. Instead, I was frustrated by my exhaustion. I missed racing.

Exactly one month later, I went on a ten-minute run. It was brutal, but I slowly improved. And by the end of track season the following spring, I finished in the top five in the 5,000-meter run at the conference championship. I was thrilled to be back at the top of my game.

The following September, as I was gearing up for my second cross-country season at college, I returned to the doctor's office for a routine checkup. The doctor seemed distracted and excused himself from the room. I sat alone, anxiously tapping my foot on the floor.

Why am I nervous? I'm fine! I told myself. I waited for what seemed like an eternity. When the doctor returned, he looked at me and began, "Johanna, I have some news. . . ."

My heart skipped a beat.

"I'm afraid your tumor has returned," he said.

I felt like a vacuum had sucked all the air out of my lungs. I fell back into the chair, horrified, terrified and completely confused.

"This doesn't make sense," I cried. "At my checkup two months ago, you said I was fine."

"You were, and that's partly what concerns me. This tumor is growing fast."

I felt sick. I closed my eyes and took a deep breath. *How will I get through this?* Then my competitive instincts kicked in. *Come on, you can do this!* I told myself. *You never wimp out when you run. Don't wimp out now!* But this was harder than any race, because I knew I could win races.

On the way home, I prayed, "Please help me, God. I'm really scared. Am I destined to die young? Please, Lord, give me strength."

The next day I nervously stepped into the locker room to talk to my teammates.

"How'd the appointment go?" asked Julie, all chipper and clearly expecting good news. My silence told her otherwise.

"What is it?" Julie asked, rushing to my side. Other girls gathered 'round, too.

I bit my quivering lower lip in an effort to keep from crying. "I . . . I got some bad news," I told them. "It's another tumor," I said, almost in a whisper.

Everyone remained silent and motionless. Some girls covered their mouths with their hands; others just stood with gaping mouths and tearful eyes.

Salty tears rolled down my face. "I have to do intense radiation treatments," I explained. "Five days a week for six weeks."

"Oh, Jo!" Julie said, pulling me close and hugging me tight. "I'm so sorry!"

A part of me wanted to just collapse in Julie's arms and

let go of my burdens, my fears, my pain. But I didn't want to unload my problems on my teammates.

"When do treatments start?" Jane asked.

"Immediately," I replied. "Why?"

"You don't think we're gonna let you go to treatments alone, do ya?" Jane said.

"No way! We'll all take turns driving you," Julie chimed in.

I was shocked—but utterly touched—by their offer. "But it's seventy miles to the hospital in Rochester," I said.

"So what?" said Colleen. "We're a team. We stick together."

I couldn't believe it. I was floored by their generosity. A sense of relief washed over me. I had a long road ahead, but I knew I could face it with friends like these to lean on.

The next six weeks were horrible, as radiation treatments beat me worse than any opponent ever did. I was weak, tired, nauseated, and—once I started training—very slow. But several months later, in February, I was feeling tougher, faster and more energetic. I was psyched up for track season, and my friends welcomed me back with open arms and kind words. I'll never forget a conversation I had with Julie one day before practice.

"Johanna, there's something I've been meaning to tell you," she said. "You're the strongest person I know. After watching you, I've learned that anything is possible. You've taught me to have faith."

I could feel my cheeks redden with embarrassment. "I have?"

"Yeah. No matter what life throws at me, I know I can overcome it and become a stronger person. I know that from watching you."

Julie's words humbled me. "Don't be so impressed," I said as I pulled my hair back into a ponytail. "I used to take God for granted. It was like, I knew he was there, and that seemed like enough. But when I got sick, I prayed a lot more. As my body grew weaker, my spirit grew stronger."

"Were you ever angry with God?" Julie asked.

"I was at war with my illness, not with God," I said. "How could I be mad at him? He gave me the strength and stamina to fight. He also gave me a new perspective on life. Getting sick made me extra thankful for my family and friends."

"Are you scared another tumor will grow?"

I leaned down to tie my shoe. "I don't want to waste my time worrying about something that may or may not happen," I said. "Besides, God wants me to live for today by appreciating and using the gifts I have now. And that's precisely what I'm going to do."

I finished tying my shoe and looked at Julie.

"C'mon," I said. "Let's go run."

Johanna Olson
As told to Christy Heitger-Casbon

[EDITORS' NOTE: *Johanna graduated from Luther College and is currently running with TEAM USA Minnesota, a group of elite runners who are training professionally. She's also pursuing a master's degree in applied sports science and hopes to one day coach at the collegiate level. During a doctor's appointment this past August, Johanna was given a clean bill of health.*]

Let There Be Faith

The recess bell pierced through the school and into the blue afternoon sky as children were scrambling to get out and onto the playground that held so many imaginary adventures. The tire swing, always a favorite, had the attention of just about everyone in the third-grade class. Kids pushed each other with the assurance that falling was not an option. Only the boisterous laughter of the children could be heard above the rusted squeak of the swing.

These are the days I remember at Trinity Lutheran School, when our best friends were the kids who chose us first to be on their kickball team or who would trade a Hershey's chocolate bar for an apple. Kristie, an accident-prone tomboy who was everybody's friend, was in my pint-size class all the way from kindergarten to eighth grade. We did everything together from going to confirmation class to playing on the aging swingset together.

Growing up together, we made the transformation from a small sheltered Christian school to the much more intimidating high school. Kristie made all the changes look effortless. She made friends easily, and her involvement in athletics and extracurricular activities made her the captain of many teams and, eventually, class president. Her days were filled with numerous English papers, wondering about that cute guy in math class and running laps for "voicing her opinion" in volleyball practice.

In our Christian school, we were always taught to believe—both in God and in ourselves. With only one week to go before junior prom, this insight was challenged when doctors found a tumor behind Kristie's eye. Kristie was diagnosed with cancer at the age of sixteen. The sudden discovery brought waves of shock and sadness to the lives of everyone who knew her.

With a 50 percent chance of survival, she started chemotherapy treatments that forced her to continue her education at home. Morning, evening and night were spent in the hospital with IVs pumping through her veins. As she laid in that unfamiliar place losing her hair, her appetite and her energy, the rest of us continued our lives. She feared losing her life, while we wrestled with the fear of not being asked to the prom.

As she battled cancer, I never saw Kristie cry. I never saw anger flash across her blue eyes. I never saw hope fade from her heart. And not once did I ever see her point a finger at God or blame Him for what happened to her. Yet, many times I saw the strength and faith she carried within her. It shone so brightly that nobody could look at her and imagine she felt as much pain as she did. She had faith. And it showed through her smile, her heart and her soul. She was determined to win the battle that God had prepared her for.

Kristie was an inspiration to us all. At such a young age, she proved that she could handle a life-threatening illness with a smile on her face. She believed that God would see her through, and she believed in her own strength. In the end, I always said that the reason God chose Kristie to conquer this obstacle in life was because He knew that she could handle it. God told her "let there be faith," and she embraced it with all she had.

Lindsay Beth Wondero

[EDITORS' NOTE: *On Christmas Eve 2000, Kristie's cancer came back, and she had surgery in January. She is currently undergoing chemotherapy. She is in our thoughts and prayers.*]

A Cross in the Sand

For where your treasure is, there your heart will be also.

Matthew 6:21

I wasn't abused as a child. I just felt, well, lonely, neglected and unloved. I don't think it was my parents' fault necessarily. I just wasn't a happy kid.

My family did not attend church. I had never even set foot in one. We weren't rich, but we had enough money to take a beautiful trip to Florida every Christmas. Of course, my parents loved to tease me about Santa not doing address changes very well. But every year packages marked "From Santa" made their way to our motel room.

One morning in Florida, I had decided to play in the warm, white sand with my shiny new pail and shovel. My parents weren't going to the beach, so I settled for digging in the motel courtyard. I looked at the sandy field, sparsely covered with tropical weeds. I set out to find the best spot to create my sandy masterpiece. I chose a place way out in the middle, sat down contentedly and began to dig.

About four inches down, my shovel clinked on something. I was always dreaming of finding lost pirate treasures or being the first one to find an unopened genie bottle. Therefore, it wasn't a stretch for me to think I had hit the jackpot. However, my little shovel had uncovered a treasure of a much different sort. It was a small, silver cross. I turned it over and over in my hands, looking at it as the sun made it glow brightly. Etched on the back of the cross were words I could just barely make out: "Jesus Christ is Lord." I wasn't sure what that meant. I never showed anyone the cross, but kept it hidden as one of my prized possessions, only taking it out when no one was around. To me, it wasn't just a cross; it was a sign.

During high school, I was a typical teen. I sought out fun and trouble, but rarely got caught for it. My life was going downhill fast, but I thought it was perfectly under control, except for the emptiness inside that I couldn't account for. Sometime during my sophomore year, I decided I wanted to know about God.

Most of the church services I attended with my friends were good, but one was life-changing. As the music began to play, I was consumed, and I felt Him. He was the One I had been searching for. He was the One who had been calling me. The pastor called for those who didn't know Him to come forward. I couldn't have stopped my feet if I had wanted to. He prayed, I prayed, and my life was never again the same. I went home and wept with joy. A seemingly lifelong void was finally filled. For some reason, I am quite sure my search began the day I hit metal with my little shovel and found a cross that said, "Jesus Christ is Lord." Now I no longer have to dig to find my treasures. All the treasures I'll ever need are just a prayer away.

Lana L. Comstock

Wise Guy

When I was thirteen, I found out that Jesus was not born on Christmas day. Billy Hollister, who was always reading history, told me that.

When I argued with him to the point of rage, he made me go into his house where he had a lot of books and look it up. Historians said that Jesus was born in the early spring, probably March, because that's when the Romans collected taxes and that's when his parents would have had to return to their native city to pay them. Billy Hollister's book said that their native city was not Bethlehem at all, but probably Nazareth.

All of this confused me and made me sad in a way I can't explain. I liked the idea of Jesus being born in Bethlehem and in the winter when it was cold and dark and everyone needed some good tidings of great joy. The spring just seemed wrong somehow.

I kept this information to myself until the Christmas when I was fourteen and Aunty Dan came to visit. Aunty Dan came to live with us for a while each winter because she was getting on and her own house was fast becoming a chore for a woman living alone. My mother, who loved her very much, wanted her to stay with us permanently, but Aunty Dan would not hear of it.

She always arrived looking very tidy. Beneath her small black felt hat, her white hair was braided and coiled in a bun at the back of her neck. She carried a very small black suitcase, worn at the handle, and always wore a dark blue dress with a white collar and her best black Chesterfield coat when she came for a visit. She had a very big laugh for such a little woman and liked to play word games.

One night at supper she reminded us all that it was about to be the birthday of Jesus Christ. "I think we should remember that when we give each other gifts," she said.

I missed her point completely—presents were important to me, after all. Besides, I wanted to show off my knowledge of history. So I told her that December 25 was not the birthday of the Lord. Everyone looked up at me as though I'd crawled out from under a rock.

Aunty Dan lowered her eyes for a moment, fussed with her napkin and then looked at me with an expression of such sorrow that I wished I had kept my ideas to myself.

We were all sort of subdued that evening, and I went to bed early to think about things. After my parents came to kiss me good night, I read for a while by the light of my flashlight. Just as I was about to drift into sleep, my door opened and Aunty Dan came into my room and sat on the edge of my bed.

"You have a lovely and inquisitive mind, darlin'."

I don't know what I expected her to say, but certainly not that. I thought I was due for a lecture of some sort. What she said to me really got my attention.

"I've been thinking about the question you brought up about Jesus' birth. You know, there are several months in which scholars believe that holy day could have happened. Many think he was born on January 6, in fact." She patted my hand with hers. Her fingers felt soft and very warm.

That she knew such things astonished me. I figured she just accepted what everyone believed because it was the thing to do.

"The truth is that it doesn't matter one bit. It only matters that he came to us. And the only important thing about that wonderful moment is that it divided time forever. There is the time before he came to teach, which was a brutal and forlorn world, and the time after, when he showed all mankind by his love that it was possible to live in grace and light and goodness of spirit. For most of the world, time itself has been divided ever since. Now we speak of the time before Christ's birth and the time after he came. I think that is a mighty accomplishment, don't you?"

I started to stammer out something, an objection maybe. Then she said, "Time and dates have nothing to do with important things like love and truth and compassion. You know that in your heart; I am sure you do. That is the message to remember, and it hardly matters on what day you remember it."

And with that, she folded my hands into hers, kissed me on the forehead and left the room so quietly I did not even hear the door close.

Walker Meade

"Now remember, Jesus, you just ate lunch
so no walking on water for at least twenty minutes."

Childish Faith

*F*aith is not belief without proof, but trust without reservation.

Elton Trueblood

"Chrissy! Chrissy! Abby's gone!" My seven-year-old
brother Matthew pounded on my bedroom door. Flinging
it open, I found myself gazing into his frantic eyes. "We
looked everywhere," Matthew cried. "What if she got outside? Abby's never been outside alone!"

Fear ran down my spine as I thought of the little black-
and-white kitten we'd brought home only three days
before. Abby was supposedly a family pet, but Matthew
had formed a special bond with her. Now, as I stared at my
brother's tear-streaked face, I felt my heart break. He had
lost his new best friend.

"Don't worry. We'll find her," I said, trying to sound like
a reassuring big sister. A tiny creature like Abby could be
lost almost anywhere.

I led Matthew downstairs where we joined the rest of
the family in turning the house upside down. We searched

through closets, under couches, inside potted plants and anywhere else a kitten might hide. I kept praying that Abby would suddenly leap out and pounce on our ankles, but she never showed up.

"She must be outside," I told Matthew. "Let's go look."

"You'll never find her out there," our older brother, Anthony, informed us. "She's probably been eaten by a hawk or squashed in the road by now." Sometimes he could be negative.

"Hush up!" I snapped, throwing him a sharp look. "Don't listen to him," I told Matthew. "Abby's fine."

"Okay," Matthew replied. But I could tell he didn't believe me.

Together, Matthew and I searched the soybean fields that surrounded our house. We slithered under the porch. We checked every tree in the yard. The sun set, and there was still no sign of our kitten.

"Will she be okay?" Matthew asked me, as I tucked him into bed that night.

"I don't know," I sighed. I had spent the entire evening trying to convince my brother that everything would be fine, yet I could no longer hide my disappointment. I was sure we'd never see Abby again.

Now Matthew tried to cheer me up. "We'll find her," he said, suddenly confident. "I'm gonna pray that Jesus lets her be here in the morning. How's that?"

That's crazy, I wanted to say, but I didn't. Instead, I tucked the covers under Matthew's chin. "Go ahead and pray," I said, "but don't get your hopes up."

I tried not to show how doubtful I was, but Matthew saw right through me. "Jesus cares about kittens, too," he insisted.

To make Matthew feel better, I knelt and listened to his simple, childish prayer. It was sweet, but it was obvious we'd been reading my brother way too many of those

Christian bedtime stories in which children were constantly praying for and getting miracles. He had a lot to learn about the real world.

"Is Matthew asleep?" Mom asked when I came downstairs.

"Yeah," I replied, staring at my feet. I missed having Abby chew on my socks.

"Oh, by the way," I added, "don't be surprised if your son doesn't believe in God in the morning."

"What do you mean?" Mom asked, surprised.

"Well, Matthew just prayed that God would send Abby back by tomorrow, and he really thinks it's going to happen."

"And you don't?"

"Oh, please!" I exclaimed. "I'm not seven years old, Mom. I know God's not a genie in some lamp you just rub and make a wish to."

"No," Mom agreed, "but He still cares about everything that concerns His children, no matter how small."

"Sure, Mom," I replied. "I'll remember to tell Matthew that when he wakes up tomorrow and his kitten isn't waiting to play with him."

As I stalked out of the room, I heard my mother sigh. "Oh, Chrissy," she whispered softly. "What's happened to your faith?"

I tossed and turned trying to fall asleep. Visions of Abby's whiskered face and Matthew's trusting eyes swam through my head, along with my mother's lingering words. *What's happened to your faith?*

I rolled onto my stomach. I remembered when I was a child, how I used to pray about every little thing, from a broken toy to a rained-out picnic. What was it that I had back then that made me so quick to turn to God and so certain that He cared? Was it really ignorance, or was it faith?

I yanked the blanket over my head, trying to block the questions from my mind. After all, these were questions I had worked hard at erasing from my mind a long time ago. I wasn't going to allow a kitten to bring them back.

I woke up early the next morning and rolled out of bed. I needed to be up in time to run damage control when Matthew realized his kitten was gone for good.

Suddenly, I felt something pounce on my foot. There was Abby, staring at me with her shining, green eyes. She let out a playful "meow" and tugged at my sock.

I lifted the tiny kitten in wonder, rubbing her furry face against my cheek. As happy as I was to find Abby safe, I was a bit overwhelmed. I felt guilty that I had spent half the night refusing to have faith that God would bring our kitten home.

Matthew!

Cradling Abby in my arms, I ran out of my bedroom and across the hall, where my brother was still asleep. Setting Abby on Matthew's stomach, I watched her crawl across his chest and place a tiny paw on his cheek. Finally, he opened his eyes.

"Abby!" he yelled, throwing his arms around his precious pet. "Oh, Abby, I knew God would find you! Didn't I tell you, Chrissy? Didn't I?"

"You sure did," I said, smiling.

"Now we need to thank Him," Matthew reminded me. "We have to thank Jesus for taking care of our Abby."

Matthew bowed his head and folded his hands, one finger resting on Abby's tail. Now humbled, I followed his lead. I realized that although I was much older than my little brother, there was a lot I could learn from his innocent faith.

Christina Marie Dotson

In-VINCE-ible Lessons

Just looking at my vivacious, seven-year-old brother, Vincent, no one would know the painful struggle he went through just three years ago, nor would they know about the invincible way in which he fought and overcame his terminal disease.

"Mommy, my leg hurts," Vincent said three years ago. Having used all his energy to limp to the couch, he laid down for a rest. For a very busy four-year-old who never sat still, this was not normal. His sudden inability to walk up or down stairs and go about his usual playful activities concerned us. My family thought it might be an injury from roughhousing with my other younger brother. The doctor said it was his left hip and advised temporary bed rest, which seemed to help at first.

Soon it was time for Vincent's Halloween party at pre-school. The children formed a parade circle outside the school to show off all their cute costumes. When an adorable panda trailed far behind the rest of the class as they walked around, we were abruptly reminded that something was seriously wrong.

It's been three years since Vincent was diagnosed with neuroblastoma, a fast-growing malignant childhood cancer.

The cancer in his abdomen had already spread to other parts of his body, including his left hip. The day I was told, I was overwhelmed with confusing emotions. I saw how young, innocent and weak Vincent looked, and all I could do was watch and hope. I prayed that he could handle chemotherapy, surgery, radiation and two stem-cell transplants.

Even through his pain, loss of hair, mouth sores, isolation from friends, stomach cramps and other complications, Vincent never complained. He continued to enjoy the simple things of childhood—jokes, arts and crafts, teasing and goofing off. As the months went on, Vincent's smile and sense of playfulness remained. Vincent made me feel more secure that God would protect him and be there through everything.

Vincent made it through a number of treatments and both his bone-marrow transplants. However, following his three-month isolation period at home, Vincent came down with post-transplant kidney problems. After a six-day hospital stay, he was stabilized and able to still go with us on his Dream-Come-True trip to Disney World. My family received our dream come true, as well. Vince was clear of cancer and finished with his treatments. Within five months his kidneys were 90 percent healed. Vincent has proven himself invincible. He is now almost three years cancer-free and still maintains a wonderful, spirited attitude. We are so thankful to God that he is a survivor.

Vincent taught me important lessons through his suffering. Not only did I learn to trust in God, but also that the Holy Spirit and His gifts will always be here for me in times of spiritual or emotional challenge. Patience, the presence of God and an inspirational little boy have made an everlasting impact on my life.

Casey Glynn Patriarco

[AUTHOR'S NOTE: *My brother is still surviving. He is almost eight years old, and I hope one day he will read this.*]

2

ON COMPASSION AND FORGIVENESS

Blessed are the merciful, for they shall obtain mercy.

Matthew 5:7

Lantern

In ninth grade, I transferred from my small church school on an island in the Puget Sound to the public high school. At my old school, everyone kind of got along. There weren't any cliques, and although there were a few kids with learning disabilities, they were accepted—no one was an outsider. I had heard that public school could be tough socially, and I was determined to fit in. So I did my homework. I studied a yearbook from my new school and figured out what kind of clothes the popular girls wore. I studied the way the cheerleaders styled their hair, and I got my hair cut the same way. I was actually looking forward to going to what I thought of as a "real" school.

I thought I was prepared, but I was in for the shock of my life. The new school had a big-time pecking order, and everyone knew exactly where everyone else was. There were the popular kids at the top of the status ladder—the cheerleaders and the football players and their friends. Then there were the middle-rung kids—not popular, but not picked on either. Then, at the bottom of the ladder, were the total outcasts. They were called "scums." I did not want to be a scum.

There was this one boy named Eric Spangler who was at the very bottom of the social ladder. He was a pale, skinny redhead with a big nose and nerdy glasses. He was very intelligent, got all A's and was super nice, but everyone picked on him for no reason. Well, I guess there was a reason—the way he looked. His family was poor and couldn't afford to buy cool clothes for their kids, so Eric and his siblings always wore weird, outdated stuff from thrift stores.

Eric was allergic to perfume, so one of the jocks would spray some on him on an almost-daily basis. He'd have to go take a shower and come back wearing gym shorts, his skinny blue-white legs sticking out like a bird's. Eric was so unpopular that his last name became an insult—instead of calling someone a "scum," they would call you a "Spangler."

My new clothes and hairstyle didn't make me the instant friends I had hoped. The popular kids could somehow tell I wasn't one of them. I looked right, but they sensed something about me, like wolves that can tell by your scent you aren't one of the pack. I decided to join the Christian club on campus before I ended up like Eric. The leader of the group was Cindy, a pretty blonde girl with freckles. Cindy warned me to tuck my small gold crucifix inside my collar so people wouldn't call me a Jesus Geek. The kids in the club were socially "middle rung," as I'd come to think of it. I didn't seem to have much in common with them, but it was a relief to have people to eat lunch with. Eric always sat at a big table all by himself.

I began noticing this punk-rock girl around campus. We only had three punk rockers on the whole island, and she was the only girl. She had hair the color of cherry Kool-Aid and wore black clothes and matching nail polish. She was pretty quiet and kept to herself. At lunch I'd see her reading in the library or walking by herself across the football field. She wasn't a popular kid, but she wasn't a "scum" either—she had a certain look in her eyes that stopped people from picking on her. I asked the kids in the Christian club who she was.

"Oh, that's Lauren Meyers," Cindy said. "She's a Satanist."

"What do you mean?" I asked.

"Well, just look at her."

I didn't say anything. I was starting to feel a little uncomfortable with the other kids in the club. They were always putting people down.

I passed Lauren in the halls a couple times. She had a very calm, self-assured way of walking and looking at people. I wondered what made her carry herself with such confidence. It didn't look like she had any more friends than Eric Spangler.

One day a couple of the cheerleaders poured a whole bottle of perfume on Eric. He screamed and tore at his clothes. "It's not funny! I can't breathe!" he yelled, gasping for air.

Everyone stood around laughing at him. I felt a knot in my stomach. I wanted to stop them, but my feet were frozen to the floor. Then I saw Lauren pushing her way through the cheerleaders. She shouted, "What are you doing? Can't you see he's really sick?" and led him to the nurse's office.

Someone snickered, "Eric has a new girlfriend."

"Dude," someone else said, "Lauren's a Spangler now."

Eric ended up having to go to the emergency room, but he was okay. I was so ashamed of myself for avoiding him. I decided I'd start saying "hi" to him in the hall. I began talking to him a little bit, too, but only when no one was looking. I really liked him, but was terrified someone would see us together and call me a "scum" or a "Spangler." Then the worst thing happened. Eric asked me if he could join the Christian club. I felt paralyzed. I wanted to be nice to Eric, but I sure as heck didn't want him in my club. So what could I do? Tell him no right to his face? Instead I told him we had to ask Cindy because she was the president.

"We're full," Cindy told him. "We aren't accepting any new members right now."

Eric looked crushed, but he just said, "Okay, I understand."

"How come you said that?" I asked after Eric left, even though I knew.

"It's hard enough being a Christian without someone like that in our club," she said.

I felt horrible. How could we call ourselves Christians and then reject someone who wanted to join us?

When I got home I burst into tears and confessed to my mother. I thought she would say she was really disappointed in me and give me a big guilt trip, but she didn't.

"God loves you even when you do a bad thing," she said. I shook my head, and tears streamed down my face. Mom just smiled and lit the kerosene lantern that we kept around in case of storms. "You see this lantern?" she asked.

"Yeah."

"What do you notice about it?"

"I don't know." I looked at it. The glass was covered in soot. "It's kind of dirty."

"Yes. But it still burns brightly inside," Mom said. "You and Eric, even the kids who poured the perfume on him, you're all like this lantern. You all shine a bright light. God can see it even if you need to clean the glass."

I thought that this was a pretty story, but I didn't see how it related to the situation. I did decide to drop out of the club. Maybe I wouldn't have any friends, but at least I'd be able to live with myself. I would have liked to have made a big speech about why I was leaving the club, but

I didn't have the guts. I just stopped showing up.

After I quit the club, I ran into Lauren in the hall one day, and she said, "Hi."

"Hi," I said, and kept walking. I felt shy. I thought she was a nice person because of what she did for Eric, but I didn't picture us ever being friends. We were so different. I also wondered if she was saying hi to me just to be nice like I had to Eric.

The popular kids had stopped dumping perfume on Eric since he went to the hospital, but they found other ways to torment him. One day, I turned the corner of the gym by the football field and saw a group of guys stuffing Eric in a garbage can. Then I saw a blur of cherry and black running across the field toward the guys. It was Lauren to the rescue again. Something changed in me right there, and I felt a surge of courage.

"Hey!" I shouted at the boys. "Leave him alone!"

They were startled and let Eric go. He climbed out of the can and ran away.

Lauren reached us, out of breath. "Why do you do that?" she asked them, her clear, confident eyes drilling into the boys.

They looked uncomfortable. I thought they would start making fun of her, but instead one of them said, "I don't know."

"Well, think about it," Lauren said.

Without discussing it, Lauren and I walked away together, leaving the stunned boys behind us. "So, you want to eat lunch?" she asked.

"Sure," I said. "But I think you should know I'm a Christian."

"What makes you think I'm not?" Lauren laughed.

"Um . . . I guess the way you dress."

"I don't care about the way you dress. Why should you care how I dress?"

"I'm sorry. I just thought you wouldn't think it was cool to hang out with a Christian."

"Do you think Jesus was cool?"

"What do you mean?"

"I mean that a lot of people didn't like the company he kept, but he didn't let that bother him."

"Yeah, that's true. He just did what he believed was right, no matter what."

"That's what I try to do." She wasn't bragging or anything; she was being matter-of-fact. "It makes me feel free."

What Lauren said really shook me. Now I understood where her confidence was coming from. I remembered what my mom had said about the sooty lantern. I realized that Lauren just had a cleaner glass than I did. I finally understood that when I was rejecting others based on their appearance or social status, I was really rejecting myself. From that day forward, I vowed to never forget my light.

Hallie Lantana

An Unexpected Customer

Every person is Christ for me, and since there is only one Jesus, that person is the one person in the world at that moment.

Mother Teresa

I had barely made my way around the counter when I saw her.

The moment I established eye contact, a huge smile spread across her face. As the corners of her mouth curved upward to form a lopsided grin, her eyes came alive and danced with light. I smiled back and asked, "Is there anything I can help you with today?"

In an excited, childlike tone, she exclaimed, "My name is Didi!" I watched as she fumbled around in her pocket. After a few seconds the search ended, and she presented me with a tube of lipstick. "I need one of these. Do you have one of these? I need a new one of these."

As I took the lipstick from her dirty hands, I knew my coworkers were staring my way. It was not difficult to conclude what they were thinking. After all, Didi was not our typical customer. Her clothes were slightly wrinkled. Neither of her two shirts was tucked in, and no two articles of clothing even remotely matched. Over her blonde, unruly hair she wore a blue baseball hat. Curls peeked from beneath the hat, framing her face.

Although she must have been in her mid-twenties, she acted as if she were a young child. The faces of my co-workers communicated relief in being spared the chore of assisting her, while also revealing the humor they found in watching me take on the challenge.

Feeling slightly uncomfortable, I answered, "Yes, we have that brand. They're right back here." As I led Didi to the back of the store, she walked steadily beside me and asked, "What's your name?"

Once again I smiled and answered, "My name is Ashleigh."

"Ashleigh," she repeated. "That's a pretty name, Ashleigh. You're nice, Ashleigh."

I was unsure how to react to Didi. Politely, I replied, "Thank you."

Upon reaching the back of the store, I attempted to subtly reclaim a portion of my personal space. Moving slightly to the left, I examined the lipstick Didi had handed me earlier. As I focused my attention on it, the temptation to run overwhelmed me. And why not leave her there? After all, there was nothing wrong with allowing her to look for the correct shade. I had shown her where to look and had been friendly. Why should I stick around and continue to feel uncomfortable? Didi would be fine on her own. How hard could it be to match a lipstick shade?

Nearly convinced by my reasoning, I opened my mouth to excuse myself. Before I could form the words, conviction washed over me. Deep down I knew I did not have a good excuse to walk away. Yes, I could justify my reasoning, probably well enough to convince both myself and others. But I realized that no line of excuses or justifications would make it right.

I couldn't simply walk away and leave Didi to search for the lipstick on her own. I was basing my decision to leave Didi on what I saw—a woman who was less than what the world said she should be. I had failed to view Didi through the eyes of Jesus. When Jesus looked at Didi, he didn't see someone of little value or see an uncomfortable situation that he couldn't wait to escape.

I suddenly recalled stories in the gospels where Jesus reached out to and loved those who society rejected and counted as worthless. He loved the beggar and the blind man. He embraced the tax collector and the harlot. He extended healing to the lame and the leper. Jesus recognized and treated each individual as a precious, priceless soul.

It didn't take long for me to locate the correct shade. Removing it from the shelf, I handed the tube to Didi. "Here you go. This is the one."

Excitedly, Didi took the tube from my hands and asked, "This is the right one?"

"Yes, this one will look pretty," I answered as I led Didi to the front of the store. As I reached the counter, I knew my coworkers were still watching me. Yet, this time I was not bothered by their expressions. I saw Didi through new eyes. I no longer focused on her dirty hands or less-than-perfect attire. I saw Didi as I believe Jesus would, as someone made in the image of God.

After I rang up her purchase, Didi smiled at me and said, "Ashleigh, you're sweet."

I simply smiled back, knowing that, because of Didi, I would now view my world just a little bit differently.

Ashleigh Kittle Slater

A Lesson in Lavender

To err is human, to forgive divine.

Alexander Pope

For as long as I can remember, Easter Sunday has been my favorite day to go to church.

I was almost always able to smuggle a few pieces of Easter candy into the service, and the way I saw it, anything is tolerable if you're munching on malted milk eggs and chocolate bunnies. Even church.

I also liked the fact that on Easter there was usually more singing than preaching at church. The music of Easter is great—lots of "Hosannas" and "Alleluias"—and it's much more uplifting than most sermons.

Heck, just watching our church choir was worth the price of admission—from that hangy-down thing that wobbled on the underside of Ione Merrill's arm while she led the choir, to the way Stan Smith's whole head turned purple as he strained to reach the highest tenor notes.

But the best thing about Easter was the impromptu fashion show that took place as members arrived wearing their Easter finery. For those few minutes, the girls and women in our congregation were supermodels, and the church aisle was their runway.

And the most super of the supermodels was Ginger MacDonald, one of the eldest and most respected members of our congregation. Tall and stately with bright red hair, this beautiful woman commanded attention even in a plain black dress (tastefully accessorized, of course). But on Easter she stole the show, with colorful outfits and huge hats that could have been spotted from space.

Especially on the Easter of the lavender hat.

Actually on that Easter, Ginger's entire outfit was lavender, including lavender shoes and gloves, a sweeping lavender dress and a lavender purse the size of a small continent. But it was her lavender hat, complete with lavender veil, that got my attention. It couldn't be helped—Ginger and her hat were sitting right in front of me.

It was shaped like a satellite dish, with the bottom brim extending down the back of her pew almost to my knees. I couldn't even cross my legs without bumping the hat, and that prospect frightened me. If I bumped it, it might tumble off her head, and who knows how many people would be crushed if that thing started rolling? I couldn't see and I couldn't move, but I could eat, so I focused my attention on the goodies in my pockets.

I unwrapped the first treat and popped it into my mouth, and without thinking I put the empty wrapper in Ginger's hat. I wasn't trying to be malicious. It's just that this big lavender dish was right there in front of me, and it seemed like the thing to do. I continued eating candy and stashing the wrappers in the lavender trash receptacle until it was time for the choir to sing. By this time, there was a good-sized pile in there, and it startled me when it started to move. I tried to grab the wrappers, but it was too late. They were now part of an otherwise all-lavender Easter ensemble.

Those who hadn't seen Ginger smiled and nodded as she grandly made her way to her place in the choir. Smiles turned to giggles, however, when she walked past and revealed the pile of garbage in the back of her hat.

Ginger seemed unaware of the stir she was causing until a well-meaning choir member scooped the wrappers out of her hat and handed them to her, whispering a word of explanation. To her credit, Ginger's pleasant expression never changed, but I was sure I could see mayhem in her eyes as she sought me out and fixed me with her oh-so-charming gaze.

I prayed fervently, but God chose to ignore my pleas to make the choir's song last forever. When the song ended and choir members began returning to their seats, I braced myself for the reaction I knew was coming.

Instead, Ginger looked at me, smiled and winked, then she picked up her big lavender purse and put the wrappers in it. And she never mentioned the incident again. I learned an important lesson about forgiveness that day— a lesson in lavender.

And what better day than Easter for a lesson like that?

Joseph B. Walker

The particularly unruly animals
oft were banished to Noah's Dinghy.

Sweet Sixteen

When you blame others, you give up your power to change.

Douglas Noel Adams

"Hurry and get dressed, Shelly." Mom's overly cheerful voice penetrated the closed door to my room. "The sun's shining. Let's go riding!"

Mom knew I was on the phone with my boyfriend. The last thing I wanted to do on that Sunday afternoon was go horseback riding with my mother. Yet, I dared not argue back, not after our blowup the night before. *I'm sixteen years old!* I seethed. *Why can't she just stay out of my life?*

Sometimes, I hated my mother. I desperately wanted her to give me space. She sponsored my cheerleader squad. She came to every one of my volleyball and softball games. She even taught at my school. Wherever I went, there she was. As if that weren't bad enough, she was always ordering me around. When I was little, I liked it when Mom was protective and when she got involved in my activities. But now I wanted more independence, a chance to make my own mistakes.

Truth is, in spite of Mom's constant surveillance, I managed to break most of the rules at our private Christian school. And the more I rebelled, the more Mom clamped down. The more she clamped down, the more I rebelled.

Take the night before, when we had the blowup. Okay, so I *was* a few minutes late coming in. Well, maybe it was more like an *hour* late. Anyway, just as I expected, Mom followed me into my room. "Where were you all this time, Shelly? I worry about you when you're late. *Anything* could have happened! Why didn't you call me?" On and on and on.

As usual Mom threw in a little scripture for good measure, as if she didn't drill me on memory verses at our breakfast table *every morning!* "Remember, Shelly," she'd said that night, "the Bible says, 'Children, obey your parents. . . . If you honor your father and mother, yours will be a long life, full of blessing.'" Then, she added, "Shelly, your life just shortened by one day!"

"Mom!" I yelled. "Will you just leave me alone?" When she finally left, I slammed the door behind her.

Today she was pretending nothing had happened, trying to make us look like the ideal, loving family of her dreams. Meanwhile, after hanging up the phone, I was sitting there thinking, *What is all this horseback-riding business? Mom isn't even a horse person! She just wants to know what I'm doing every minute.*

Halfheartedly I pulled on my riding boots, then went over to the dresser. Reaching for a comb, my hand brushed against the necklace Mom had given me for my last birthday. *I'd better wear this or she'll ask where it is.* Reluctantly, I fastened the silver chain around my neck and straightened the pendant—the silver outline of a heart with its message, in script, suspended inside: "Sweet Sixteen."

By the time I got to the barn, Dad had already saddled

our horse, Miss CharDeck—we usually called her Charcey—and Mom was swinging into the saddle. "Mom, *what* are you doing?" I shrieked. "You've never ridden Charcey before! She's a *big* horse." *I cannot believe this woman!* I thought. *She'll do anything to be part of my life. And I just want her out of it!*

While Dad was bridling the Arabian, Babe, Mom discovered her stirrups were too long. Before Dad could turn around to adjust them, Charcey charged away at full gallop.

Scared and inexperienced, Mom probably reacted by doing all the wrong things. Whatever the reason, Charcey was out of control. I had never seen that horse run so fast, her mane and tail flying in the wind. It was as though she had to show off what a quarter horse is bred to do: win short-distance races. With every stride of her powerful haunches, she gained speed.

I watched, horrified, as Charcey's hooves beat at the earth, faster and faster like something possessed, a thousand pounds of straining muscle thundering across the pasture. With lightning speed, Charcey reached a corner of the pasture fence—a place of decision. Should she jump? No. Too high with a ditch on the other side. Other choice? Make a ninety-degree turn. Charcey turned. Mom flew high into the air, crashed through a barbed-wire fence and landed on the sun-parched ground.

Then nothing, except for Charcey's hoofbeats as she tore back to the barn.

Dear God! No! No! This can't be happening! I sprinted across the pasture, outrunning Dad on the Arabian. "Mom! Mom!" *Please, God, don't let her be dead! I didn't mean it, God. I don't really want her out of my life! Please!*

The barbed wire was holding her in an almost kneeling position. Her right wrist and hand dangled the wrong way, her neck and head were turned as if broken, and blood oozed from gashes on her back. *Is she breathing?*

Please, God, she thinks I don't love her. "Mom?"

After what seemed an eternity, I heard a moan, then a weak, "I'm okay, Shelly."

"Mom! I didn't mean to be hurtful. I love you, Mom." Ever-so-carefully, I began untangling her hair from the barbed wire, barely able to see through my tears. "Oh, Mama, I'm so sorry. I'm so sorry."

"I know, Shelly," Mom somehow managed, while I made one last tug on her now-shredded pink sweater and freed her from the wire.

"We've got to get you to the hospital," Dad said, jumping back astride Babe and turning her toward the barn. "I'll call an ambulance."

"No," Mom said, and because she was a nurse, we listened. "You can carry me in the van."

It wasn't easy, but we did it. Dad barreled down the highway. Meanwhile, I did what Mom had taught me—I quoted scripture, the first one that popped into my head. "Rejoice in the Lord always," I said, close to her ear. "And again I say rejoice." For once, I must have done the right thing, because Mom, through all her pain, started quoting scripture, too, one verse after another, all the way to the hospital.

Mom spent most of the next three months in a wheelchair, and during that time the two of us did a lot of talking. "Mom," I told her, "I know I act a lot like Charcey did that day of the accident. I just want to charge through life without being held back, not missing anything."

"Yes, Shelly, and I always want to be in control, to make sure things go right. To protect you from getting hurt."

We decided because we were very different, we'd probably always clash over one thing or another. We agreed on something else, too. That we loved each other, no matter what.

Still, I felt a need to do something more to make things right. One day at school I asked permission to speak at our chapel service. Standing on stage at the microphone, I took a deep breath and started. To the other students, to the faculty and especially to Mom, who sat in the back of the room in her wheelchair, I said, "I want to apologize for all the mistakes I've made this year, mistakes that have hurt others. Worst of all, they have hurt my mom."

I told them how hateful I had been to my mother, how I had yelled at her to stay out of my life. Then I told them about Mom's accident, about how, at the thought of losing her, I realized she is my very best friend, and that she only wants the best for me. "Please, you guys," I begged my fellow students, "tell your mother you love her. Don't wait until it's too late, like I almost did."

I looked back at Mom who was beaming, while dabbing at her eyes with a tissue. "Mom," I said, voice quivering, "I ask you to forgive me. I ask *God* to forgive me."

As if on cue, one of Mom's Bible verses popped into my head. *"'If we confess our sins, he is faithful and just to forgive us our sins.'" Thank you, God, for believing in me, even when I disappoint you over and over.*

Just like Mom! I realized in a flash of insight. Instinctively, I reached up and caressed the silver pendant at my neck. My fingers traced the intricate lettering, "Sweet Sixteen." *Sixteen? Yes. Sweet? Hardly! But I will try, Mom.* I smiled through my tears. *I will try.*

Leaving the platform, I became aware of a new-for-me feeling, one that said, *It's okay, Shelly, to let your mom into your life.*

Even when you're sweet sixteen.

Shelly Teems Johnson
As told to Gloria Cassity Stargel

Only Words

You can speak well if your tongue can deliver the message of your heart.

John Ford

My father is a triathlete. That is, he has competed in several triathalons—a kind of marathon that includes running as well as swimming and bike riding. He's been doing it for years, and he really enjoys all the sports, but his favorite is bike riding. Ever since I was little, I've always loved going biking with my dad. We would leave the city behind and follow the bike trails way up into the woods of Wisconsin. We had a favorite spot where we would picnic. It was always our special time, and it kept me in great physical shape.

But as I grew older and became a teenager, I was distracted by other things to do with my time. Suddenly, it was very important to go shopping with friends or to a movie with a boy. I saw my dad every evening at home. Why did I have to devote my free Saturdays to all-day bike trips with him, too?

If my indifference hurt him, he never let on. He never asked me outright, but would always let me know when he was planning a bike trip in case I wanted to come.

I didn't, and as I approached my sixteenth birthday, I wanted to spend less and less time with my dad. Except for one thing—I didn't mind being with him when he was giving me a driving lesson.

More than anything else, I wanted that driver's license. It meant freedom. It meant no more waiting for parents to pick me up. No more carpools. It meant looking cool behind the wheel of a car as I drove past my friends' houses. Of course, since I didn't have my own car, I would still be dependent on my parents, since they were allowing me to use theirs.

It was a Sunday morning, and I was in a terrible mood. Two of my friends had gone to the movies the night before and hadn't invited me. I was in my room thinking of ways to make them sorry when my father poked his head in. "Want to go for a ride, today, Beck? It's a beautiful day."

But I preferred to sit in my room and stew. I wasn't very polite when I said, "No! Please stop asking me!" It didn't matter that he hadn't asked me in months. Or that he was trying to cheer me up. It didn't even matter that he just wanted to be with me, as I knew he did.

"Leave me alone!" That was what I said. *Leave me alone.* Those were the last words I said to him before he left the house that morning.

My friends called and invited me to go to the mall with them a few hours later. I forgot to be mad at them and went. I came home to find the note propped up against the mirror on the mail table. My mother put it where I would be sure to see it.

"Dad has had an accident. Please meet us at Highland Park Hospital. Don't hurry, just drive carefully. The keys are in the drawer."

I grabbed the keys and tried hard not to speed or cry as I drove.

When I reached the hospital, I went in through the emergency room. I remembered the way because I had been there once before when I broke my arm. I thought about that incident now. I had fallen out of the apple tree in our backyard. I started to scream, but before the scream was out of my mouth, there was my dad, scooping me up, holding me and my injured arm. He held me while my mother drove us to the emergency room. And he held me as they set my arm and put a pink cast on it. I do remember the pain, but I also remember how safe I felt in my dad's strong arms. And I remember the chocolate ice cream afterward.

I saw my sister Debbie first. She told me our mom was in with our dad and that he was going up to surgery soon. She said I had to wait to see him until after the surgery. Just then, my mother came out.

She looked very old. I burst into tears without saying a word, and she put her arms around me.

My father's injuries were extensive. He had been riding on the sidewalk and, as he approached a stoplight, it had turned green. He had the right-of-way, but the white delivery truck making the right-hand turn didn't think so. At least, the sixteen-year-old driver didn't think so. Later, he admitted that he never saw my dad because he didn't look in his outside mirror.

The only reason my dad wasn't killed is that he ran into the van; the van did not run into him. He smashed head and face first into the side of the truck. His fiberglass helmet absorbed the blow, but he broke both shoulders and his left clavicle. The doctors put him in a horrible metal brace that attached to his body with screws. It braced his head and neck and looked horribly painful. My mom forewarned me about this apparatus before she let me see my dad because she was afraid that the sight of him would freak me out. She was right.

Still, as my mom said, it could have been much worse. My dad never lost consciousness. This proved to be a very good thing because the shaken boy who drove the truck wanted to move my dad, to help him up. Even I know you don't move someone who has been injured like that.

"Your father was able to tell the kid to leave him alone and just call 911, thank God! If he had moved Daddy, there's no telling what might have happened. A broken rib might have pierced a lung. . . ."

My mother may have said more, but I didn't hear. I didn't hear anything except those terrible words: *Leave me alone.*

My dad said them to save himself from being hurt more. How much had I hurt him when I hurled those words at him earlier in the day?

I had to wait until the next afternoon to see him. When I did, he was in terrible pain. I tried to tell him how sorry I was, but I couldn't tell if he heard me.

It was several days later that he was finally able to have a conversation. I held his hand gently, afraid of hurting him.

"Daddy . . . I am so sorry. . . ."

"It's okay, sweetheart. I'll be okay."

"No," I said, "I mean about what I said to you that day. You know, that morning?"

My father could no more tell a lie than he could fly. He looked at me blankly and said, "Sweetheart, I don't remember anything about that day, not before, during or after the accident. I remember kissing you goodnight the night before, though." He managed a weak smile.

I never wanted him to leave me alone. And to think it might have happened. If he had been killed, we all would have been left alone. It was too horrible to imagine. I felt incredible remorse for my thoughtless remark.

My English teacher, a very wise woman, once told me

that words have immeasurable power. They can hurt or they can heal. And we all have the power to choose our words. I intend to do that very carefully from now on.

Becky Steinberg

"I never really believed that Satan was active in our world today until I tried to drive a car with a clutch."

Dance Lessons

The weak can never forgive. Forgiveness is the attribute of the strong.

Mahatma Gandhi

As the last few seconds of the homecoming football game ticked away, I stuffed my French horn into its case as quickly as I could and looked around for Dale, my date for the dance. I still couldn't believe that the top musician, track star and president of our class had asked me. But where was he now? I scanned the other bleacher sections and spotted him hurrying down the steps on the far side. I waved and he called, "You'll still be ready in a half-hour?"

I nodded, but I wanted to answer, "I've been ready for two years, from the day we met as ninth-grade science lab partners." We were both in the same crowd from band, so I'd been sledding with him, to movies and parties, on skit and float committees—but I was just one of a dozen girls he considered his friends.

At the start of our junior year, though, Dale and I ended up sitting together in the orchestra pit for a musical, and we were assigned to do a joint history project. A few study sessions later, he asked me to homecoming. *Me!* For four weeks, we'd walked between classes together, walked home together ... the whole school knew we were together.

The evening unfolded just as I'd dreamed. Dale arrived right on time to pick me up, and we headed to a great seafood restaurant. He grinned as we sat down and said, "Let me order tonight."

By candlelight, we dined on crab cakes, chowder and lobster. I tried to wave aside dessert, but Dale said, "You have to try one of their tortes. We'll share."

Trading bites and laughing as we swapped school stories, I kept thinking what a great year it was going to be at Dale's side for band trips, Snow Dance and prom. Sadie Hawkins, the girl-ask-boy dance, was just a few weeks away. I put down my fork and asked, "So, what are you doing on the twenty-first?"

Dale looked blankly at me. "For what?"

"Sadie Hawkins. You'll go with me?"

"Uhh ... Myra already asked me."

I almost choked. Myra was a good friend of mine. She must have asked him at the football game when he disappeared toward the end. Come to think of it, they'd talked after band all week. What an idiot I'd been! Dale probably wished he was with Myra right now. I managed to mumble, "I hope you two have a good time," as I chased a chocolate crumb across my plate.

The waiter brought our check. I stared at my napkin, thinking, *God, how can this be happening? How can I show my face at school again?*

Then Dale made the strangest sound. When I looked up, Dale's face had taken on the greenish tint of our school cafeteria walls. "What's wrong?" I asked.

Dale stood up, checking his pockets. "My wallet. I must have left it at home."

Revenge! And I hadn't had to do anything. Oh, how I'd enjoy watching Dale try to explain this to the manager. After all, the whole band probably knew by now that he'd been with Myra at the game.

But a voice inside me said, *And you call yourself a Christian?* I had enough emergency money from my father to cover the bill. I knew the voice was right. I pulled the wad of bills out of my purse and let Dale pay the waiter.

But I didn't have enough cash left to get us into the dance. I wondered about calling it quits for the evening, but I knew it would be easier to talk to my friends Monday if I at least appeared at the dance. We drove to his house in silence.

Dale took me inside and introduced me to his parents. His dad asked, "Why aren't you at the dance already?"

Dale looked at his shoes. "I forgot my wallet."

"You what? Of all the irresponsible, foolish . . ." His dad went on in that tone for a good five minutes. Dale did his best to melt his six-foot frame into the carpet. Finally, he managed to grab his wallet, and we made a dash for the car.

Once inside, Dale leaned back for a moment and shook his head. At that point I calculated that he and I were about even on the humiliation scale for the evening. I said, "Hey, we could be scraping lobster shells and congealed butter off our plates back at the restaurant."

He looked at me, then said, "I've sort of blown this evening for you, haven't I?"

He said it just like any friend would, this guy who had been a good friend for more than two years. And suddenly I knew I still wanted to be friends. And I knew somehow I had to forgive him—and Myra, too. I said, "Well, we'll still get there in time, unless you manage a flat tire or something."

He laughed as he started the car, saying, "At least I know the gas tank is full."

By the time we got to the dance, we were back where we started—good friends. I was so cheerful I even told Dale to take a few dances with Myra.

Some of my friends couldn't believe that I could still study with him. Or that we did skits together at parties. Or that I didn't care who he took to Snow Dance or prom. Maybe it was just a bit of a miracle that his forgotten wallet urged me into forgiving him right then and there.

Jane Kise

3

ON KINDNESS AND GIVING

But love ye your enemies, and do good, and lend, hoping for nothing again; and your reward shall be great, and ye shall be the children of the Highest.

Luke 6:35

The Mirror

Do nothing from selfishness or empty conceit,
but with humility of mind let each of you regard
one another as more important than himself.

Philippians 2:3

At fourteen, I was the new girl at a rural school in an apple-orchard valley. There were twenty-eight kids in my class, which was equally divided between boys and girls. It was the tightly knit group of twelve girls that kept me an outsider. They teased me about my bright red hair, my height, my clothes, my shoe size, my accent and anything else they could think of. I cried myself to sleep after my parents' pep talk. They said all the right things like "Give it time" and "Once they get to know you, they'll love you." I wanted to believe them, but the evidence proved otherwise.

Then, a few months into the school year, my parents' predictions came true. I was playing out in left field for the girls' baseball team when a ball rocketed right at me. I put my mitt up as a shield, and the ball packed itself right into my glove. That play saved the game, and we beat the boys' team for the first time. Well, after that, the girls couldn't just exclude me from the victory party. It turned out they liked my sense of humor, and a few actually said they wished they had my mass of auburn hair. Suddenly, I was "in." Friendships grew, and soon I was included in the overnights and birthday parties.

Spring break came and went, and we returned to a school of freshly waxed floors, redone bulletin boards and one new girl. Rosa was petite and quiet. Her family had come to work in the apple orchards. I knew how she felt, so I smiled at her and helped her find her way around. The final weeks of school passed, and we came to our last day and the traditional eighth-grade graduation dance.

I decided it would be a nice gesture to invite Rosa over to help her get ready for the dance. It was fun getting ready together and being each other's support when those insecurities would creep in.

We stood side by side in front of the mirror.

"Oh, thank you, Cindy!" Rosa said. We smiled at each other's reflection. "I only wish my friend Tracie could see me now. I wish she could come to the dance. She said she's never gone to one. She made me promise to have the best time ever and to remember every moment so I could tell her all about it tomorrow. She was so excited for me."

Tracie! I had never even thought of her.

Tracie was one of the fourteen girls in our class. I was so happy when the twelve welcomed me into their inner circle that I had never looked back or looked around. I never looked at or thought about Tracie, the one who stood alone until Rosa had become her friend.

That night at the dance, Rosa was a hit. It was great to see her so happy. Yet I couldn't stop thinking about Tracie. For the first time I was aware of her absence. Tracie didn't make it to the dance that night, but she affected me more than anyone who did. Tracie's example of wanting her friend to be happy even though she had been excluded far outshined me taking such pride in a small kindness to another. I might have done a nice thing, but for whose gain did I do it?

These moments when we are humbled enough to learn are when God really teaches us. That night I learned my own happiness is only part of the big picture. I learned it is just as important to make sure others are loved and accepted as it is to feel that way ourselves.

Cynthia M. Hamond

A Father's Love

Let your light so shine before men, that they may see your good works and glorify your Father who is in heaven.

Matthew 5:16

His name was Brian, and he was a student at the small high school I attended. Brian was a special-education student who was constantly searching for attention, but usually got it for the wrong reasons. Students who wanted to have some "fun" would ask, "Brian, are you the Incredible Hulk?" He would then run down the halls roaring and flexing. He was the joke of the school and was "entertainment" for those who watched. Brian, who was looking for acceptance, didn't realize they were laughing at him and not with him.

One day I couldn't take it anymore. I told the other students I had had enough of their game and to knock it off. "Aw, come on, Mike! We're just having fun. Who do you think you are, anyway?" The teasing didn't stop for long, but Brian latched onto me that day. I had stuck up for him, and now he was my buddy. Thoughts of, *What will people think of you if you are friends with Brian?* swirled in my head, but I forced them out as I realized God wanted me to treat Brian as I would want to be treated.

Later that week, I invited Brian over to my house to play video games. We sat there playing video games and drinking Tang. Pretty soon, he started asking me questions like, "Hey, Mike. Where do you go to church?" I politely answered his questions, then turned my concentration back to the video games. He kept asking me questions about God, and why I was different from some of the kids at school. Finally, my girlfriend, Kristi, pulled me aside and said, "Michael, he needs to talk. How about you go down to your room where you can talk privately?" My perceptive girlfriend had picked up on the cues better than I had.

As soon as we got to my room, Brian asked again, "Hey, Mike. How come you're not like some of the other kids at school?" I wanted to tell him about the difference God had made in my life. I got out my Bible and shared John 3:16 and some verses in Romans with him. I explained that God loved him just the way he was, and that He had sent Jesus down to Earth to die on a cross, rise from the dead and make it possible for everyone, especially Brian, to spend eternity in heaven if they believed. I didn't know if he was comprehending what I was telling him, but when I finished explaining, I asked him if he wanted to pray with me. He said he would like that.

We prayed together: "God, I know I'm a sinner, and that even if I were the only person on Earth, You still would have sent Your Son down to die on the cross for me and take my place. I accept the gift of salvation that you offer, and I ask that you come into my heart and take control. Thank you, Lord. Amen."

I looked at Brian and said, "Brian, if you meant those

words you just prayed, where is Jesus right now?"

He pointed to his heart and said, "He's in here now."

Then he did something I will never forget as long as I live. Brian hugged the Bible to his chest, lay down on the bed and let the tears flow down the side of his cheeks. When I cry, my sobbing is very loud, but Brian's was unearthly silent as the emotions he'd held inside let loose. Finally, he said, "Mike, do you know that the love God has for me must be like the love a husband has for his wife?"

I was floored.

Here was someone who had trouble comprehending things in school, but had now understood one of eternity's great truths. He lay there for another five minutes or so as the tears continued to flow.

I still remember the incredible feeling I had at that moment: a high higher than anything a substance could ever give, the high of knowing that God works miracles in everyday life. John 10:10 immediately came to mind: "I have come that they may have life, and have it to the full."

About a week later everything came into perspective for me. Brian really opened up to me. He explained that his dad had left him and his mom when he was five years old. As Brian stood on the porch that day, his dad told him he was leaving because he couldn't deal with having a son like him anymore. Then he walked out of Brian's life and was never seen again. Brian told me he had been looking for his dad ever since. Now I knew why the tears kept flowing that day in my bedroom. His search was over. He found what he had been looking for since he was five years old: a Father's love.

Michael T. Powers

The Stutterer

Music is well said to be the speech of angels; in fact, nothing among the utterances allowed to man is felt to be so divine. It brings us near to the infinite.

Thomas Carlyle

I had asthma when I was thirteen—and bad eyes. I guess the combination made me an easy target. I wasn't a particularly great student, but I wanted to go to college and I was willing to work hard to get there.

The neighborhood I grew up in had a lot of gangs. It was hard to stay clear of them. Getting into a gang meant you had to beat up somebody. I was the "somebody" for this one kid, Juan. As I was walking home one day, Juan attacked me. He kicked and punched me until I was unconscious. I guess that was enough to get him into the gang, because he didn't kill me.

What he did do was leave me with a brain injury that resulted in a stutter. Getting over a stutter is not easy, but it is not impossible, either. All through high school, I learned techniques for relaxing and thinking through what I wanted to say to avoid stuttering. Singing is one of these techniques. I discovered that I had a love for singing. And I was good at it!

I sang in my church choir and got a lot of solos. Mrs. Keefe, the organist, offered to teach me some music theory so I could really get a message across when I sang gospel music. I loved it!

I was offered a scholarship to a college with a great music department. I had once thought of becoming a nurse, but dreams change. Music had become an important part of my life, and now I thought about becoming a professional singer or a music teacher. One of my teachers told me about the field of music therapy. In the spring of my freshman year, I took a course in music theory that required clinical time spent in a children's hospital.

On my first day at the hospital, I was introduced to the family of an eight-year-old girl who had had a brain injury as the result of a car accident. The little girl, Shauna, couldn't see or speak, although she could make some sounds. The doctor assured us that she could still hear. I didn't know what I was supposed to do for Shauna. After all, I was only eighteen, and this was my first assignment.

I began by playing all sorts of music for Shauna. I tried to find things I thought an eight-year-old would like, such as N'Sync, the Backstreet Boys and Britney Spears. She seemed to like the music, but she made no progress in her development. I tried classical music. Then came jazz, rap and heavy metal. She really hated heavy metal, and I was relieved because I couldn't imagine having to listen to it every day.

I had just about run out of ideas when I was sitting by her bed one day, humming a tune from church. It was a song that I just couldn't seem to get right.

But something about that music was right—amazingly right! Shauna moved her arms! I knew immediately that it wasn't just an involuntary movement. It was purposeful. I opened my mouth and sang like I was in church. I sang one song after another until I ran out of ones I had memorized. Then I started singing them over and over. I spent the whole day singing to Shauna. She went down to her physical therapy, and I followed her, singing. She went to occupational therapy, and I sang to her. The nurses changed her bandages, and I sang to her.

At the end of the day, I sat by her bed, exhausted, too tired to even hum. Shauna's mother came in as she did every evening when she got off work. She took Shauna's hand and put it to her cheek.

We both heard it at the same time: "Mama." Shauna said "Mama"! If we both hadn't been there, hearing it together, we might not have believed she actually said it. Shauna's mother screamed, and two nurses rushed in. We all hugged each other!

It was a small step, to be sure. But it was a step.

I often think back on how I got into this field. I remember that I wanted to be a nurse, to help people. But the gang member who gave me a concussion and a stutter altered my path. At the time, I couldn't understand why I had to be so brutalized. What had I done to deserve a brain injury? But now I realize that if I hadn't stuttered, I would never have known how much I needed music to be part of my life, how much we all need music to be part of our lives. Music heals.

Bad things happen in life. Kids get picked on, beaten up and hurt in car accidents every day. But good things happen, too. People say they see the hand of God in events like the ones in this story.

I see it, too. But more importantly, like Shauna, I hear it.

Name Withheld
As told to Marsha Arons

"Writing hymns is harder than I thought! I can't think
of anything that rhymes with 'Hallelujah' except
'glad I knew ya' and 'we'll tattoo ya'!"

Reprinted by permission of Randy Glasbergen.

Faith Overcomes Fear

To live with fear and not be afraid is the final test of maturity.

Edward Weeks

"Allison, wake up!" my mom yelled.

The big day had finally come, and for the first time in two months I actually felt nervous. What had I gotten myself into? I was tempted to pull the covers up over my head and drift back to sleep. But instead I tore myself out of bed and began to repeat my prayer verse over and over as I readied myself to go: "The Lord is the one who saves me. I shall trust in him and will not be afraid." I added, "Lord, you are in control of my life. Not my will, but your will be done."

As my mother and I rode the twenty-minute drive to the church, minutes seemed to stretch into hours as I tried to calm my nerves. I felt physically sick, but I knew I had to go through with this. I had worked too hard and come too far to turn back now. My mind was racing as I drifted into a daydream about how this whole experience had begun.

For many months I had been praying for the opportunity to travel on a mission trip over my summer break. My prayers were answered. As my church youth leader handed out forms for a group called Next Level Missions, I knew this was the mission for me. Although the mission departed from a church located seven hours from my hometown, and I didn't know anyone who would be going on this trip, I put aside my fear and put my faith in God that he would guide my way. I was heading to Ixmiquilpan, Mexico.

Once I had decided that I was going to Mexico, things happened quickly. I began to prepare for my trip. The finances, travel plans and all of the many preparations quickly began to fall into place. I had my heart set on this, and I wasn't giving up. Never once did I feel nervous or afraid. I kept trusting in God that this was what He wanted me to do.

However, when the moment I had so carefully prepared for finally arrived, I was terrified. Maybe because it had only seemed like a dream until now, and suddenly it was becoming a reality. It had all seemed easy before this day. As we drew closer to the church, I wanted to shout at my mom, "Turn around! I don't want to go anymore! Please just don't make me go through with this!"

But instead I remained silent as we pulled into the parking lot. There was no turning back now. I hopped out of the car with a look of confidence on my face. As I walked toward my fellow travelers, I felt like I was invisible to everyone. No one said a word to me. Had I arrived at the wrong place? I slowly pulled my luggage into the sign-up room. I looked down the list of names, and there in black and white I saw my name staring back at me. This was really it. Before we said our good-byes to our families, we joined hands to pray. I was secretly hoping I would never have to let go and that my mother could just go with me.

As I nervously climbed into the van with nine strangers, I somehow knew that my life was about to change forever.

These "strangers" turned out to be cool people. As time passed we developed friendships, and by the end of our trip we were a family. We shared everything, from tears of sadness to tears of joy. We formed bonds that could never be broken. We learned that even though we were all different ages, from different backgrounds and different places, we were all here for the same reason: to serve other people in God's name.

We spent two weeks in the mountain villages of Mexico. Our group put on church services, which included dramas, puppet shows and speaking. In return, we received so much more than we gave. The people there had nothing, yet gave us everything. They opened their homes to us, fed us and lovingly provided us their homes to sleep in. The love I thought I was there to "give" was returned a hundredfold.

I was so happy I hadn't let my fear stop me from going on this life-changing journey. The passage I had heard so often now made sense: If you choose to walk in faith, instead of fear, God will use you and truly bless your life.

Allison Carlyon

"Now don't get me wrong . . . I love the idea of
'Youth Under Christ the King,' but . . ."

Care Bags

*You give but little when you give of your posses-
sions. It is when you give of yourself that you
truly give.*

Kahlil Gibran

Annie loves going to the mall with her mom and bringing home big boxes full of teddy bears, games, coloring
books and crayons. But she is no spoiled child. On the
contrary, the fourteen-year-old is one of the most generous, kind-hearted kids you'll ever hope to meet.

Annie's mom, Cathy, is a child-abuse prevention educa-
tor. Every day she talked to schoolchildren, teaching them
how to protect themselves and report abuse. At a conference she attended, a social worker asked Cathy and other
adults at the meeting to save tiny shampoos and soaps
whenever they stayed in hotels.

"Usually children who need emergency shelter come
with nothing but the clothes on their backs," Cathy told
her daughter that night. Annie knew she wanted to help
somehow.

Later, lying on her bed surrounded by her collection of Beanie Babies, books and toys, Annie thought about how safe and loved she felt. And then she had an inspiration.

"I'll collect shampoos and soaps because the kids need them," she told her mom, "but I'll also collect toys and games and other fun stuff to make them feel happy, too."

Annie contacted Children's Services, which loved her idea. She and her mom composed a letter describing her idea, and she hand-delivered the letter to local merchants.

Many businesses were happy to help. They gave Annie gift cards to buy toys, stuffed animals and books. Area pharmacies, grocery stores, hotels and dentists donated toothpaste, shampoo, packets of tissue and other toiletry items. Women's groups and schools volunteered to sew beautiful fabric drawstring and handled bags. Annie filled each bag with new items she had collected and named them "Care Bags."

She pinned this poem to the outside of each bag:

This little bag was made especially for you,
To say I think you're special, and I care about you, too.
Inside you'll find a bunch of things like toothpaste, soap or a toy,
I collected all this stuff for you to fill your heart with joy.
I hope this makes you happy, today and every day,
And remember someone loves you in a very special way.

After only a few weeks, Annie delivered thirty Care Bags, which were distributed to needy foster children and crisis-care kids throughout the city. Annie was told the children loved the care bags, and they carried them everywhere. One little boy even slept with his.

As word of Annie's Care Bags spread, other merchants began donating diapers, pacifiers, night-lights and gift certificates. Complete strangers, Girl Scout troops, 4-H clubs, schools and church groups from all over the United States began sending boxes of stuffed animals, receiving blankets, school supplies, journals and decks of playing cards. The town even gave her space in a local senior center, where donations are stored and volunteers help Annie fill the bags. A computer expert helped Annie create a Web site: *www.carebags4kids.org*, which has encouraged many others to get involved.

Over the past three years, Annie has assembled over four thousand Care Bags. Annie has never met any of the Care Bag recipients, but she knows she's making a real difference.

"It was so nice to receive something when everything was falling apart," one little girl wrote to thank Annie. "It's nice to know someone really cares."

Heather Black

"If Jesus could feed 5,000 people with only two fish and five loaves of bread, then why can't five guys figure out how to share one last slice of pizza?"

Reprinted by permission of Randy Glasbergen.

Strive

Strive for the dawn of a more gracious world,
Thrive in the vision of true joy unfurled.

Pray for the day when all men are equal,
Stay for the time when love has a sequel.

Stand for the things that you know to be right,
Understand hardships of souls without sight.

Give to the people who have less than you,
Live to give credit where credit is due.

Endure rocky friendships; forgive and forget,
Ensure that the needs of the nation are met.

Hope for the time that leaves nothing to mourn,
Cope with the trials of change as they're born.

Fight for the wounded in body and heart,
Unite the cultures long-since torn apart.

Speak for the people who haven't a voice,
Seek for the option to be given a choice.

Exist for the chance to right wrongs old and new,
Resist any force that defies what you do.

Strive for the dawn of a more gracious world,
Thrive in the vision of true joy unfurled.

Anastasia Cassidy

4

ON LEARNING
AND HEALING

*T*ake good hold of instruction and don't let
her go: Keep her, for she is your life.

Proverbs 4:13

A Forgiving Heart

Thursday afternoon was turning out to be anything but beautiful. The day started right as Trevor began his morning on his knees in prayer. The day became more challenging until finally school was out, and Trevor went home.

The door slammed, and the sound of footsteps clomping up the stairs caught his mother's attention. "Trevor?"

"Yes, Mom." Although detecting that "I'm miserable" sound in his voice, his mother didn't say anything, knowing Trevor would soon be down to talk. She was right. Ten minutes later, Trevor walked into the kitchen and plopped down in a chair.

"Mom, you remember that boy, Robby, that I told you about?"

His mom nodded.

"Well, we got into a fight today."

"Oh, Trevor."

"Wait, Mom, it's nothing like that. I sat next to him in third period. He kept pushing my books onto the floor and poking at me. I just sat there and said nothing. After the bell rang, I walked out into the hall and he pushed me. When I turned, he said, 'You must think you're real cool 'cause you're on the football team.' I turned and started to walk off. He shouted, 'Are you too good to fight me?' I responded, 'I don't want to fight you.' He stood in front of me and, with a bunch of other kids standing around watching, he said, 'If I hit you, you won't fight back?' As I turned away from him, he hit me. I just looked at him. He waited for me to hit back, but I just said, 'Feel better?' and walked off. He didn't follow me."

"You did the right thing," Trevor's mom said. "God will take care of the rest."

By Saturday morning, Trevor was less bothered by what had happened with Robby. In fact, Robby had been extremely quiet on Friday and didn't even look at Trevor.

Trevor told his mother, "I'm going over to Steve's to see if he wants to go canoeing."

Halfway to Steve's house, Trevor saw a Chevy with its flashers on. As he passed by, he noticed a person working under the hood. Trevor turned around and pulled up next to the car. Getting out of his truck, he walked up and asked, "Do you need help?"

The guy slowly turned. It was Robby.

Trevor swallowed hard as he walked closer to the car. "What seems to be wrong?"

Robby stood there, amazed, then told Trevor what his car had done. Trevor was mechanically inclined, and the boys worked together for over an hour, not really saying much.

With the car finally running, Trevor said, "Well, see you around."

"Wait!" Trevor turned to see Robby's hand extended. "Thank you, Trevor."

"You're welcome." Trevor felt God leading him to add, "What are you doing today?"

Robby couldn't hold eye contact with Trevor when he said, "Nothing."

"Ever been canoeing?"

Robby looked at him with a smile. "I used to go with my dad when I was younger."

The two headed toward the river and were soon floating with the current. "Hey, I'm sorry about the other day, Trevor."

"Don't sweat it. It's no big deal."

Robby continued, "It's just, I see you in school and you seem so different, you know, happy all the time."

Robby told Trevor how his stepfather had beaten him after his real dad died. Robby said he used drugs as a way of escaping reality. His stepdad finally walked out, but darkness and despair still surrounded Robby. He explained his plan of suicide that would have taken place that very afternoon.

Robby dug into his pocket and pulled out a note. It read, "I have reached the end; desperation and loneliness have won. I can't change my life and have given up trying. I doubt anyone will miss me. I write this not as a cry for help, because it's too late for me, but as a cry for hope, hope that someone will love the unlovable." Trevor looked up from the note to Robby, who was visibly shaken.

Trevor spoke in a broken voice, "Jesus loves the unlovable, Robby, and it's never too late for God." Trevor told Robby of the compassionate love of Christ and how it could change his life.

Over time, Robby's life changed dramatically. He gave his life to Christ and began to rely on God more and more. The two boys now share their faith with anyone who will listen and have put together a Bible study group at their school. They are always there for each other, even on the most challenging of days. They know there's nothing that canoeing down the river with a best friend can't cure.

Gary Flaherty

Desperate to Fit In

Be yourself. Who else is better qualified?

Frank J. Giblin

I'm not exactly sure when I realized my life was spinning out of control. I'd grown up in a Christian family. I thought I had my act together—until I hit high school. That's when things started happening, things that led to some major changes in my life—and some bad decisions on my part.

First, we started building a new house, and the only time we could work on it was on weekends. We stopped going to church regularly. Eventually, we spent less and less time praying and reading the Bible.

Second, my best friend moved away the summer before I started ninth grade. I felt really lost and alone, so when school started that fall, I was desperate for some new friends. And it was that desperation—my intense desire to "fit in" with the right group—that ultimately led me down the path of self-destruction.

I met Kathy during the first week of ninth grade. She

was one of the most popular students, so when she befriended me, I was pretty excited. I'd never been part of the "in" group before.

It wasn't long before Kathy invited me to spend the night with her at another friend's house. But that night turned out to be much more than I'd expected. It was a major party, with lots of alcohol.

I'd never been to anything like that before. And before the night was over, I started feeling excited about everything—the sense of freedom, of having no limits, of trying something new and grown-up.

I didn't get drunk that night, but a pattern had begun. Before long, I was partying and getting drunk every weekend. I was staying out later and later. And since our house was still under construction, we didn't have a phone. So I would stay out as late as I wanted, then I'd lie about where I'd been. What could my folks do? They couldn't say, "Well, you should have called."

By that time, I wanted to be as thin as the other girls in my group of friends. So I started forcing myself to throw up after meals. In fact, I became so obsessed with my weight that when I was at a party, I'd drink until I'd get sick and throw up, just so those calories wouldn't be in my body.

And then there was shoplifting. Since it was a part of the "fun" my friends were into, I felt I had to join in, too. I enjoyed the thrill of getting away with it. At first, I mostly took small things that didn't cost much. But soon, I was taking clothes and other expensive items.

So there I was, a freshman in high school, a common thief with a drinking problem and an eating disorder. And all because I wanted so badly to "fit in."

As much as I loved being part of the in-crowd, I knew my life was out of control. I wanted things to change, but I couldn't do it on my own. If I said I wanted to change, my friends would immediately dump me. But secretly, I wanted to get caught. I felt that would be my only way out.

Then it happened.

First, my folks found the wine bottle. My mom and I were up all night yelling and fighting.

Then I got caught shoplifting. The cops came and took me away in the squad car. I had to call my parents to come and get me at the police station. The ride home was awful. My mom and dad sat together in the front seat, holding hands and crying. I sat by the window, staring outside, not believing what had just happened.

How could this be? I wondered. I felt so ashamed.

Shortly after that, one of my friends caught me throwing up. She called my parents to tell them. Even though I was angry at my friend for squealing on me, it was the best thing anyone did for me. My mom confronted me, and we really had it out that night. At that point, my mom realized my problems weren't going to go away on their own, and that I was really putting myself in danger.

My mom made an appointment for me to see a counselor, and I thought it was a good idea. Those counseling sessions helped a lot. We talked about the drinking, the stealing, the bulimia, my friends, how I was feeling and what I wanted my life to be like.

I later learned how much my folks had worried about me and loved me through all the garbage I was doing. I found out my dad had been getting up at four o'clock every morning to pray for me. I cried when I heard that.

I knew I needed to make some changes in my life. I wanted to stop the drinking and throwing up and stealing because I was scared for my health and safety.

Also, I wanted to stop living a lie. I'd been lying to my parents all along. I'd been lying to my friends about what kind of person I was. And I'd been lying to myself about what was important to me. I was ashamed of the way I'd been living, and I knew it wasn't what God wanted for my life.

I had some big fears about changing, though. I knew I'd have to find some new friends who wouldn't pressure me to act a certain way. I was so afraid I'd end up with no friends at all. But God was already working on that. Within a short time, I met a group of girls who accepted me and cared about me for who I was. They also shared my Christian values, so I was free to be myself.

A couple years have gone by. I'm not interested in the party scene anymore. My shoplifting days were done after that run-in with the police. And after a lot of counseling, I'm no longer fighting my eating disorder—although I still struggle with how I feel about my body.

I'm so much happier now. I'm hanging with a good group of friends, people who love me for who I am—not for somebody I'm pretending to be. And even though I care and worry about my old friends, I've decided not to spend time with them. I've learned the hard way that I can't handle it very well.

When I last saw my old friends, one of them asked me, "What happened to you? You used to be so much fun at parties, but we never see you anymore. You should hang out with us again."

I just smiled and said, "No, thanks. I'm much happier now."

Colleen Holmes
As told to Jake Swanson

Sharon's dad knows how to turn any subject
into a lecture on sex, drugs and alcohol.

Reprinted by permission of Randy Glasbergen.

Michael

With every deed you are sowing a seed, though the harvest you may not see.

Ella Wheeler Wilcox

It's lunch hour, and the cafeteria is a zoo. At a round table near the edge of the room, I'm brown-bagging it with six of my friends. We almost always sit together at the same table in the same seats.

Lunch hour for us is a safe and predictable routine. There's never any stress or worry about where we'll sit, who we'll sit with or what we'll talk about.

But across the way, a guy named Michael sits alone. Every day. I've never seen him sitting with anyone. For that matter, I've never seen him walking in the hall with anyone, talking to anyone between classes or hanging out with anyone after school.

I only see Michael alone.

Michael is tall and thin. His shoulders sag. He walks slowly. His brown hair is straight and long. His face looks sad and hurt. Michael doesn't hide his loneliness very well.

Michael is in my P.E. class. He is not athletic. He can't throw well, he runs awkwardly, and he obviously doesn't enjoy the class. By the end of the semester, after being laughed at and ridiculed by nearly everyone, Michael's face begins to look more guarded. He seems to be learning to hide his feelings.

When I see Michael in the hall, he seems lost and confused. Instead of going to his locker between classes, he carries all his books, so he's always dropping stuff. He walks along the wall where he can avoid all the crowds.

Sometimes I wonder if anybody ever even notices him.

Sometimes I notice, but I don't do anything about it. What does it matter, anyway? I don't have any obligations toward him. He's just another kid in school who really has nothing to do with me. Right?

My youth director wouldn't agree. His big themes this year are, "Reaching Out to Others," "Being a Good Christian Witness," "Stretching Beyond Your Comfort Zone," stuff like that. My youth director talks about it all the time, challenging us to be the kind of people he knows we are capable of being.

I have no problem with these ideas. Hey, my close friends are from different faiths and backgrounds. I tell them what I believe. Some have even come with me to youth group. Isn't that reaching out?

But how could I even begin to reach out to Michael? I didn't even know if he would want me to.

Halfway through the year, while I sat in the lunchroom with my friends, I glanced up and noticed Michael sitting alone—again. And I realized I wasn't really reaching out or stretching beyond my comfort zone.

Silently, I pleaded with God to leave me alone, to not bug me about Michael because surely there was someone else who could befriend him. For me, it would be so inconvenient, so uncomfortable, so embarrassing.

But God didn't leave me alone.

And so after a few miserable days, I walked into the lunchroom. I walked past my table of friends, without telling them what I was up to. And I sat down across from Michael.

My heart was pounding. My face was burning. I felt like everyone was staring at me. And for some reason, I was afraid.

I said, "Hi."

Michael said nothing.

I said, "How are you?"

Michael said nothing.

I wanted to shrivel up and die, but I ate my lunch and made small talk while Michael just ate his lunch in silence.

I did this the next day and the next. Soon several days had passed, and I was beginning to feel a little resentful because, after all, I was doing my part. I was reaching out. I was talking about school and classes and stuff. But Michael was not doing his part by being grateful or friendly or nice.

The next week, I no longer saw Michael in the lunchroom. His schedule changed, and now he had fifth-hour lunch.

So my lunches with Michael ended.

I went back to sitting with my friends. We talked about school and classes and teachers and what we'd do after school or over the weekend. They never pried about the whole Michael thing. I just told them it seemed like maybe he needed a friend.

Michael never stopped me in the hall to say thanks. He never acknowledged the fact that, for a few days, we were lunch partners. He never said I really changed his life and now he's a brand-new person because someone took the time to reach out to him. I have no idea how he felt about the whole thing or if he even noticed me.

But as I think about it, I realize that I've learned something important.

God is asking me to be a better person all the time, in all kinds of ways, even ways that aren't obvious at first. It isn't always easy, comfortable or fun. But when it's the right thing, I know what I need to do.

With this experience I learned that doing the right thing doesn't always come with an obvious reward or even recognition. But knowing inside that you did what you knew was right, even though it was uncomfortable, is all the recognition you really need.

Jake Swanson
As told to Crystal Kirgiss

Blindness

Lydia was a smart girl, very smart. She loved being with her friends, going shopping and doing what every other girl likes to do. There was only one internal difference that made Lydia self-conscious: She was deaf. One autumn day Lydia and her best friend were taking the train to do one of their favorite hobbies: shopping. Even though Lydia's best friend was not deaf, she spoke to Lydia in sign language all the time. The train continued to make its occasional stops when a boy, no older than fifteen years old, sat in the seat across from Lydia. Lydia couldn't help but notice how often the boy would glance over at her to watch her move her hands in rapid motions. This was one of the things that bugged Lydia the most.

"Why must everyone stare at me?" Lydia asked her best friend in sign language, trying to avoid the boy's stare. "Doesn't he realize that I am deaf? There is no need to stare at me. He is probably thinking that I am weird or disabled. I hate people who prejudge others!" Lydia had become quite upset.

The train came to a sudden halt, and the boy got up to get off at his stop. He casually went over to Lydia and started moving his hands as she had just moments before. "Excuse me, but I couldn't help but notice that you said you don't like it when people stare at you. I'm sorry I made you uncomfortable. It's just that I rarely get to 'talk' to other people on the train. I feel self-conscious and different, so I was excited when I saw you. I thought maybe we could be friends." With that, the teenager walked off the train.

Sara Torina

Have You Ever?

Have you ever wanted to dry a tear
that you knew you had made fall?
Have you ever said something
that you never meant at all?
Have you ever wanted to reach out
to someone who was in pain?
Have you ever wanted to give sunshine
to someone who lives with rain?
Have you ever wanted a chance
to go back and change the past?
Have you ever stopped to realize
that time slips by too fast?
Have you ever loved somebody
and never told them so?
Have you ever held back a question
that you really wanted to know?
Have you ever felt you might explode
from holding stuff inside?
That's when you have to make a choice
between happiness or pride.

I decided I would tell the truth
to share all that I feel.
My heart feels so much bigger now
truth was the better deal.

Kristy Glassen

Praying for Your Enemies

Prayer is less about changing the world than it is about changing ourselves.

David J. Wolpe

Last year I was put into a lower-level math class at school. The reason I was in this class had nothing to do with my intellect or math skills. I am blind. The school decided that it would be better for me to learn at a lower level because it takes me a great deal longer to complete assignments and grasp visual concepts.

The only problem with being in this class was that I was surrounded by "at-risk" students. These were kids who did not do well in school and didn't want to be there most of the time. Their home lives were obviously much different from mine, and they were constantly in trouble with the school and the law.

I remember sitting at my desk one morning, wondering what I had gotten myself into. We had already finished our lesson for the day, and the rest of the kids had begun to talk about what they had done the past weekend. I tried not to listen, but it was virtually impossible not to. I heard things in that classroom that shocked me. Even though the teacher was in the room, that didn't stop my classmates from discussing the parties they had been to, how drunk they had been and who they had slept with.

I began to dread going to math. I was tired of their swear words, their stories of drugs and violence, and their negative attitudes. Some days they would come into the room in such a bad mood that everyone could feel it. I began to resent the fact that I had to be there. One girl in particular began to eat away at my nerves. Some days I wanted to hide under my desk.

One Tuesday morning, I went to a Christian Student Union meeting before school. There was a guest speaker there that day talking to us about praying for our enemies.

I began to think about this. As I pondered the idea, I prayed and asked God how I could pray for the kids in my class. I had forgotten that they weren't bad kids; they were just lost.

At first, the prayers were mechanical. When I would hear their voices in class, I would pray, "Dear God, please bless so-and-so . . ." But as I continued, I began to think of the kids more often. I especially thought of the girl who got on my nerves the most. I began to think of her more and more, and in my quiet time at home I would ask God to bless her and the rest of my classmates.

As time went on, my classmates became more than just annoying kids to me. There was something growing inside my heart for them, something that wasn't there before. They began to feel like family, and I was learning to love them in a way I never thought possible.

I now see that praying is such a powerful act. Prayer is the most powerful tool a Christian has. When I pray for those around me, it also blesses my life, and it changes my perception of others. I realized I needed God's blessings to see the world through loving eyes. The prayers I said for others turned out to help me the most.

Julie Johnston

Mama's Lesson

My mother and I have always had a very special relationship, a bond that few people can comprehend. Ever since I was a little girl, I remember her teaching me about a mother's love: constant and unconditional. She would remind me of an old Polish proverb: The greater love is a mother's, then comes a dog's, then a sweetheart's. During my trying teenage years, specifically ninth grade, my mom was my best friend.

Everything was going great—at least it was for a while. I was a straight-A student who enjoyed school. Being an only child, I loved having a good time with classmates my age. A few weeks after my freshman year started, though, things began to change. I became the target of a bully. I don't know why; I had actually been his friend the year before. But nevertheless he made it his personal goal to make me miserable. I had always had a lot of friends, but as his daily attacks grew worse, more and more of my classmates joined him in laughing at me. I became the class joke. My self-esteem and assertiveness that I once enjoyed grew less with each passing day. I drew into myself and became timid, silently enduring his hurtful remarks.

I would climb into the car after school, look at Mama and burst into tears. I'll never forget the tenderness with which she rubbed my hand and the compassion with which she listened to my stories day after day.

I now know the pain she went through right along with me. How she cried as soon as she was done assuring me that it would get better—for she had no way of knowing if it ever really would. How she stayed up at night trying to think of advice she could give me—comeback lines to try—that would end it all. Mama never gave up. She was always coming up with solutions to my problems. Some of her advice worked; some of it didn't. But I remember it all. Mama started having a special prayer time from 11:55 to 12:45 every day—fifth period. Just knowing that Mama and God were thinking about me strengthened me.

One day, I snapped out of my self-pity when I found this letter on my desk after school:

Nicole,

As I look out your window I can see a little girl hanging out her doll clothes, a fifteen-year-old with the weight of the world on her shoulders and a young woman, successful at whatever she chooses to do with her life. The most difficult thing I have had to deal with is seeing the hurt in your eyes. But we're lucky because, for a lot of people, life is much tougher.

You are a beautiful, talented, smart, young, Christian woman. You have morals and concern for other people. These things aren't taught in school, but from a loving family and a loving heart.

Sit back, relax and know that there is some good in every day. Don't worry so much about what others think and say, but instead think about the things that make you special. You will not be remembered as being mean and hateful. You will be remembered as being pretty, caring, smart and compassionate. We all have our high-school memories. People will not remember you with negative thoughts.

You have plans, and you have dreams. Hold on to those. I know many of them will become a reality for you. No matter what you do, you are always loved. I know two very successful people who were bullied. They got through high school, and so will you!

You have everything going for you. Stop feeling sorry for yourself. That is the worst thing you can do. You've got what it takes, and we all know it.

Love,
Your Proud Mom

Her words of love and support changed everything. After that, all the bullies in the world could not have dampened my spirit. I saved her letter, and it's still part of my strength. It has helped me be a lot of what I am today. I love it most because it's from my mother.

Oh, and incidentally, the bully eventually gave up on me, and two years later he asked me out on a date!

Nicole Plyler Fisk

5

ON LOSS AND GRIEVING

*To every thing there is a season, and
a time to every purpose under the heaven:
a time to be born, and a time to die;
a time to plant, and a time to pluck up
that which is planted;
a time to kill, and a time to heal;
a time to break down, and a time to build up;
a time to weep, and a time to laugh;
a time to mourn, and a time to dance.*

Ecclesiastes 3:1–4

The Joy of Easter

Eternity. It is the sea mingled with the sun.

Arthur Rimbaud

Eight years have passed since the day I pulled into the driveway of our family home to find my life forever changed. I looked up to see our seventeen-year-old son writhing in excruciating pain in our front yard. He was so incapacitated, he was unable to tell me what was the matter.

Once at the hospital, he was diagnosed with an extremely rare and deadly cancer called Burkitt's lymphoma. Arrangements were quickly made to fly him south to Vancouver General Hospital where he could receive the care he needed. On Thanksgiving Day our family gathered together and prayed in the hospital chapel for courage and strength. Later that night, my son and I boarded the air ambulance. Looking out the small window, I could see the darkening blue sky. For a moment the beauty spared me from the fear and pain I was feeling. Then the darkness of the night sky was upon us, and everything was suddenly silent. I remembered Father Forde once saying that we could find God in nature, and at that moment I experienced just that. I felt God's presence. It was at that moment that I was able to surrender our difficult journey into God's hands.

When we arrived, the medical staff were ready and waiting, and within minutes I was told that he would not live to see the morning. I asked them to please do what they could for his pain, then I softly said, "Only God knows when someone is going to die." Judging from the looks on their faces, I was sure they all thought I was some religious nut.

Morning arrived, and he had made it through the night. Days and then weeks of radiation and chemotherapy followed. Gradually, the cancer was forced into remission. A bone-marrow transplant was his only hope, and miraculously both his older sister and younger brother were perfect matches. Soon healthy bone marrow was flowing into his depleted body.

The transplant was only a temporary success, however, and all too soon the cancer came back with deadly force. Once again, we were told that there was no chance of survival, and this time we knew it was true.

That evening in the darkness of his hospital room, my son bravely asked, "What will it be like to be dead?" I didn't know what to say. I felt so unsure. I tried to be honest and tell him what I felt or believed. I told him how each day I was glad to be alive, that I always looked forward to going to heaven, and now he would be there to greet me when I arrived. We could not talk anymore. Our words were choked by sobbing tears, but words weren't really necessary. Death was no longer our enemy. After talking about it and praying, it all took on a different meaning. It was the start of a new journey, from life to death, to eternity and to God.

The following days were spent planning his funeral,

which he called his "going-away party." He had very specific requests for this event, down to wanting balloons at his funeral. I told him that I had my doubts as to balloons, but he said, "Ask Father Forde. He'll let us have them."

He wanted to be cremated and have his ashes scattered at his favorite places. He wanted a small wooden cross overlooking the ocean at his grandparents' home in Nova Scotia that said, "Peace is seeing a sunset and knowing who to thank." I had my misgivings, but he said, "Mom, just do it. God will understand."

He was quickly slipping away from us. He had been fed by IV for months now and had waited patiently for the day that he could eat pizza again. I lost control and screamed that even the worst criminal on death row gets his choice of a last meal, and my son couldn't even have pizza! I heard his soft voice say, "Mom, I had Holy Communion this morning. I have all the food I need." I knew at that moment that all our prayers were being heard. He was no longer afraid to die, and I was no longer afraid to let him go. He had surrendered himself to God.

He died in my arms on Ash Wednesday. His last words were, "Mom, it is a beautiful day to die."

His funeral was a celebration of life. The church was full of his friends holding balloons that were to be released with prayers inside them. His ashes were scattered as he had asked. His grandfather lovingly made a wooden cross that stands facing the sea.

A few years passed before I was to visit his cross again. Walking across the moors toward the sea, I saw a man and his two small children placing wildflowers on the cross. As I approached he looked up. "Did you know the family?" he asked. My reply was joyous as I said, "This boy was my son."

I stayed for a while as we all silently watched the sun set into a crimson sky.

My eyes turned toward the engraved cross, and I took in the meaning of the words as if for the first time. My heart was full, and the moment brought tears to my eyes. It was clear to all of us who to thank for this moment, and I could hear my son saying, "God will understand."

Marion Blanchard

A Letter to Heaven

It's hard around here lately, Daddy,
Things are kinda rough.
Mom is really sick now, Daddy,
Life is really tough.
I rarely ever sleep now, Daddy,
Too many tears fall from my eyes.
Why did you have to leave us, Daddy?
It hurts to hear Mom's cries.
I know it's not your fault, Daddy,
I'm not placing any blame.
I just want an explanation, Daddy,
Why do we have to go through all this pain?
God needed you up there, Daddy,
But we really need you here.
So I'm mailing this to heaven, Daddy,
And signing it with a tear.
Why can't you come back, Daddy?
Why does God want us to cry?
Please write me back, Daddy,
Was I such a bad girl, you had to die?

I'm really sorry, Daddy,
I didn't want you to go away.
I just want you back, Daddy,
Why couldn't God let you stay?
I don't know how much longer,
I can live with you away.
My heart was torn to pieces, Daddy,
When God took you away.
Please ask God a question, Daddy,
Can't you come back, just for a while?
Please make Him understand, Daddy,
How much Mommy needs to smile.
Just know I love you, Daddy,
We really need you bad.
I know I'm asking a lot here, Daddy,
Please tell God not to be mad.
I guess I'll let you go now,
My writing's kinda blurry.
But if God says you can come back,
Daddy, could you please hurry?

April Linck

Letting Go

Now I am light, now I fly, now I see myself beneath myself, now a god dances through me.

Friedrich Nietzsche

It's been nearly six years. Many people would say I should be over it by now, but I don't think I'll ever be over my sister's death.

I was only twelve when my sister committed suicide. Jeri Lynn was sixteen. She had just started her junior year of high school when she decided to take a bottle of sleeping pills.

Six years later, I was still holding on to some of the feelings I'd kept inside since her death. I had a lot to say to Jeri. I never got the chance to tell her things I would have liked her to know. I had a need for closure, if that was at all possible.

People suggested that I write her a letter, but it never felt right for some reason. However, I finally reached a point where I had to do something to let my feelings out. So one night I sat down and wrote Jeri a letter. I told her everything I had felt since her death. I explained why I felt guilt and sadness, who I was angry with and all of the memories I was grateful for. Then I told her I loved her.

A few days after writing it, I took the letter to the cemetery. I sat down at Jeri's grave and read the letter to her out loud. Actually hearing the words made it more real.

These intentional actions were really helping. I was *doing* something in an effort to move on with my life. I knew I was doing the right thing. I wanted, though, to take this one step further. I put the letter and my heartache in four helium-filled balloons. I went back to the cemetery and just sat quietly at Jeri's grave with balloons in hand. I told myself I could sit there until I felt ready to let go. I thought of how much I loved Jeri and realized we both needed this.

When it was time, I stood up and released one balloon at a time. As each one made its way up, I could feel my heart becoming lighter. The burden of grief I carried was finally loosening its grip on me.

When I released the last one, I whispered, "I love you, Jeri." And for the first time in six years, I could love her without the pain and guilt that had for so long been attached to that love. I knew Jeri was smiling down on me. I had learned one of the most important lessons about love and life. I had learned the importance of letting go.

Kelli Czarnick

The Beauty of Rain

They lingered near the entrance,
     it seemed a line went on for miles,
Tears and sobs were heard throughout,
     so many faces, without a smile.
And so many questions filled their minds,
     not one of them understood,
How God could take Michael away,
     someone so young and truly good.
For Michael gave of himself,
     to anyone around in need,
There wasn't a day that didn't go by,
     without Michael performing good deeds.
He visited the local rest home,
     understood the hardships faced by the old,
Respected all the residents,
     and listened to the stories they told.
For he knew someday he could be there,
     standing alone in their place,
So Michael cherished their wisdom,
     and the smiles he brought to their face.

Two parents stood in anguish,
    fighting hard and trying to grasp,
How a freakish, tragic accident,
    could change their lives in a snap.
And oh how their minds filled with questions,
    and they just couldn't quite understand
How God could take their son away,
    before he grew into a man.
For Michael gave them respect,
    he never gave them hard times,
And he even did it in a way that was kind.
For he knew that someday he could be there,
    having a son of his own,
So Michael cherished his parents,
    and the comfort they gave him at home.

Classmates circled in silence,
    struggling just to comprehend,
Bewildered by the incident,
    that had robbed them of their good friend.
How in the world did it happen,
    why didn't God intervene?
Why did he have to take Michael,
    who was filled with such hope and dreams?
Who always to them was a true friend,
    and to anyone ever in need.
He didn't judge others by class,
    their color, their race or their creed
For he knew someday he could be there,
    needing someone to turn to,
So Michael valued each person,
    offering friendship so loyal and true.
There were pictures displayed all around,
    allowing everyone present to see,

Times with Michael alive and well,
    times that never again were to be.
There was Michael wearing a baseball cap,
    smiling his notable grin,
Working on his old pickup truck,
    oil streaking his chin.
One of him dressed for his junior prom,
    his tie adorned in a bow,
Another of Michael at five years old,
    building a fortress from the remnants of snow.
Pictures from such a short lifetime,
    a life that no longer would be
So many days that lay ahead,
    moments Michael would not get to see.
And the scent of bouquets of flowers,
    overpowered the much crowded room,
Offerings of sympathy for a life,
    which had ended tragically soon.
And in their grief and their sorrow,
    no one knew what they should say,
How to make some kind of sense of,
    what had led them there to that day.
And from somewhere in the distance,
    music filtered its way through the room,
A CD player was hauntingly playing,
    Michael's most favorite tunes.
How in the world could they bear it,
    how would they ever go on?
Why had God taken Michael,
    how did things go so horribly wrong?

In his hands he held Michael's Bible,
    he was to read from its pages that day,
To try and make sense of what happened,
    why Michael's life was taken away.

And as all eyes focused upon him,
    people sobbed all around from their seats,
The pastor from Michael's church,
    wondered what words he should speak.
For how could he help bring them comfort,
    to put everyone's mind there at rest,
It seemed assuredly certain,
    God was putting his faith to the test.
And there with all eyes upon him,
    hundreds standing and sitting around,
He nervously dropped Michael's Bible,
    a piece of paper fell to the ground.
All eyes watched him retrieve it,
    and for a moment, as he stood there,
He silently read the words on that paper,
    holding the writing midair.
And though it seemed impossible,
    it appeared God intervened with a plan,
For the words on that paper before him,
    had been written by Michael's own hand.
And so everyone listened intently,
    Michael's words now filling the air,
And with each word that was spoken,
    it seemed Michael himself was right there.

"Lord, I've so often wondered,
    why people have to know pain,
Why, when they need the sunshine,
    do You often send them the rain?
I've tried so hard to perceive it,
    why things happen the way that they do,
That I've often felt so hopeless,
    frustrated and furious, too.

But somehow I've come to realize,
   at last I finally can see,
That You have given me my life,
   and how I live it is all up to me.
So You can't be blamed for my sorrow,
   You can't be blamed for my pain,
And I need to stop hoping for sunshine,
   and instead see the beauty of rain.
For someday I know I might be there,
   standing happily next to Your side,
And I want to be worthy of heaven,
   and to leave only good things behind."

The pastor bowed down his head,
   and asked everyone there to please pray,
For each of them to value the lesson,
   that Michael had left them that day.
To be able to work through their sorrow,
   to pick themselves up off the ground,
And instead of living in sadness,
   choose to spread Michael's message around.
For God can't be blamed for our sorrow,
   God can't be blamed for our pain,
We can't always hope for sunshine,
   we must see the beauty in rain.
And take pride in the wisdom of knowing,
   that now he stands next to God's side,
For Michael was worthy of heaven,
   he left many good things behind.

Cheryl Costello-Forshey

Here to Stay

Cancer. Even the sound of it gives me chills, and it always has. I always felt bad for those who had it or knew someone who had it, but it never seemed real to me. That is, until sixth grade. Then it became very real, and it changed my life forever.

My best friend James was diagnosed with cancer that year. I was so scared. He found out about it near the beginning of the school year, and he was only given a 5 percent chance of making it through Christmas. James proved them wrong, though, because he did live through Christmas. In fact, he lived through all of sixth and seventh grade.

Toward the end of seventh grade, James was still receiving some chemotherapy, but he had hair. He no longer wore a hat to hide his baldness, and he was happy. But by the end of June, we were all in tears. He had relapsed.

James fought the disease with all of his might, but it spread to his bone marrow. Three bone-marrow matches were found in the national registry, but James would have to be in remission before the transplant could happen. Unfortunately, in early September, the doctors said that James's body wasn't responding to the treatments he was receiving. They started him on a new round of chemo, and we prayed that it would work.

James's body never did respond to the treatments. That's when the doctors gave him four to six months to live. When he called me and told me, I started crying. It was the only time that I ever let him hear me cry. He was so strong, though. He told me it was going to be okay. I don't know how he could have done that, but James was always strong and never let anything get him down, not even cancer.

About a week before Thanksgiving, the doctors gave James a slim chance of making it through the week. I was nervous the whole time, but Thanksgiving came and went, and James was still here.

In mid-December, however, James had a reaction to his platelet injection. He wasn't expected to make it through the night, but as usual he beat the odds. The doctors were almost sure he would be gone by Christmas, but he stayed with us into the New Year.

After that, he progressively got worse. He was in a lot of pain, and things were not looking good. On January 7, James passed away. It was the saddest day of my life. I couldn't sleep for two days. I kept repeating the same thoughts: *I will never see him again. I will never hear his voice again. I will never see his smile again.*

But I was wrong. That night I was on my bed crying when I heard something.

"Brittany," a voice said. "Brittany, look up." The voice was all too familiar. When I looked up, James was sitting on the edge of my bed. He looked the same as he always had, but he was sort of glowing.

"James?" I asked. "Is that you?"

"No," he said, sarcastically. "It's Santa Claus. Of course, it's me." I laughed, and he smiled. "That's what I like to see, Brittany. No more tears."

"But you're gone," I told him.

"No, I'm not," he said. "I'm right here."

I haven't *seen* James since that night, and I know some people think I'm a little nuts when I tell this story, but that's okay. James gave me the greatest gift that night. So much of what drives me is being afraid of losing—losing my parents, losing my friends and, most of all, losing the love that keeps me going. That night I learned. I experienced firsthand that no matter what, love never leaves us.

Brittany Lynn Jones

Dad's Gift

If you want to lift yourself up, lift up someone else.

Booker T. Washington

When I was fourteen, in a two-week period before Thanksgiving, my dad developed hepatitis and died. It was a shock to all of us. He had always been so healthy. He'd only been sick once before and had bounced back quickly.

As one of eight children, I was usually lost in the crowd. Now, however, adults sought me out to console me. They told me how much I resembled my father and what a good man he had been. There was an outpouring of love, visitors and food to our home. To be honest, the months that followed his death were quite beautiful, in a weird way. I had never felt so immersed in love.

At school, none of my friends knew what to say to me. I did have one friend who came to see me at my house the day after my dad died. She sat quietly beside me. I now realize how much courage that must have taken. Besides her, none of my other friends acknowledged my father's death. They acted awkward around me. It was a strange feeling.

Several months later, one of the cheerleaders in my class lost her father to a massive heart attack. Usually, she was in the midst of a huge crowd. She seemed alone most of the time now.

I approached her tentatively one day during lunch. "I think I know how you're feeling. My dad died a few months ago," I told her.

I didn't know what to expect. I was a little intimidated, to be honest. I didn't mix with "her crowd" too easily. They were all so good-looking and popular.

Abby looked me squarely in the face. Her eyes widened. And then she seemed to relax. We talked until the bell rang.

After that day, we chatted regularly. Sometimes it felt like we were in our own little world. We'd share stories and giggle about our dads. It felt good to have a connection with my dad through our talks. I cherished them.

The next school year a girl named Terry lost her dad. Terry was kind of nerdy. She was tall and skinny. Not even "my crowd" had much to do with her. Once again, I approached someone out of my need to have a bond with my father.

"I heard your dad died. My dad died last year," I told her.

Terry sighed, then gave me a description of her past week. I listened to her every word.

As soon as I could find Abby, I told her about Terry. Abby responded like I did. It was as if we were on a deserted island, and we had caught sight of a shipwrecked victim floating toward us.

We became a threesome. Not in a social way—we didn't really hang out together—but we snatched a few moments at our lockers and in homeroom to share bits of our dads. Just having someone who understood when we were going through a tough week was comforting.

I still have my yearbook in which Abby wrote, "Thanks for being my buddy. I needed you." Occasionally, I hear from Terry. I have continued to reach out to people who are in pain. I've received comfort for myself, too, as a result of connecting with others. Being able to reach out to others has returned blessings to me a hundredfold. I thank my dad for this lasting and life-affirming gift.

Mary Cornelia Van Sant

6

ON LOVE

Thou shalt love thy neighbor as thyself.

Romans 13:9

The World Won't Stop

To love is to receive a glimpse of heaven.

Karen Sunde

People say that a teenager's biggest fear is a broken heart. I think they're right. In past relationships I always ran, reasoning that if I didn't give anyone my heart, then they couldn't break it. But when I met Jake last summer, it was different. I fell in love with Jake the moment my eyes met his alluring smile.

We played Wiffle ball that day under the blistering afternoon sun. I tried to steal second, and I ended up pinned beneath him in the scorching sand. I'll never forget looking up to see his almond eyes shining down into mine. I instantly let down my guard. By the end of the day, we were revealing our darkest secrets while we played chicken in the refreshing ocean.

Eventually, Jake's hand found mine that day, and our lips met soon after. The monstrous waves crashed like thunder behind us, and somehow his hand fit perfectly into the curve of my waist. I'm surprised he didn't hear my pounding heart as the anxiety raced throughout my body.

As soon as I kissed Jake, I was afraid to love him. But my fears were soon replaced with a sense of security. So I gave Jake my heart and slowly fell for him.

Our personalities simply clicked, and the next few months were unforgettable. The times we shared were filled with intense talks, innocent kisses and genuine laughter. The words he spoke, no matter how trivial, always found their way to a place inside my heart.

He attempted to teach me how to play pool, and he proudly introduced me to all of his college friends. I loved how he would call just to hear the sound of my voice, making me feel as if I were the only girl in the world. My face would light up each time his car pulled up in front of my house. His car was old, and there was no mistaking the familiar sound of the rumbling engine and his blaring music. "Hey, sweetie," he would say as I climbed into the front seat.

I never questioned falling for Jake until he was no longer there to catch me. He disappeared from my life as quickly as he came. With him he took a part of my heart that I had never given before. Jake did precisely what he had promised he would never do—he left me defenseless and alone. To this day I'll never know exactly why, but Jake simply stopped calling.

Heartbroken, I found myself thinking about him constantly. I missed the scent of his clothes and the way he grasped my hand, carefully curling his fingers around mine. I missed him telling me he didn't ever want to lose me. I missed how I felt complete when we were together.

At night I would clutch my fists and bite my lip, too frightened to close my eyes because I would always end up picturing his silly grin. Every song reminded me of him. My heart wouldn't let go of the love it felt. Every time the doorbell rang I would race down the steps hoping that his familiar, loving face would be there waiting for me. My mom would walk into my room to find me staring out my window, gazing at the empty street below. Each day I concentrated on breathing, walking, talking and trying desperately not to feel.

Eventually, I began to heal my broken heart. My eyes were no longer swollen and red, and I began to accept my life without Jake in it. I slowly understood I was braver than I believed, and I was stronger than I seemed. A guy was not more important than myself. The world would not stop for my grief, and although my heart was broken, it would keep beating just the same.

The other day I returned to the desolate beach where it all began. The wind swept strands of hair across my face as the tide slowly crept up the shore line. The waves then quickly retreated, leaving behind tiny remnants of the past. Through my tears I smiled and realized that love finds people when they are least expecting it, and unfortunately it sometimes leaves in the same way. However, the memories and lessons, no matter how short-lived, remain intact forever. Love never leaves; it stays in the heart, and eventually we stop thinking about what we lost and we are grateful for what we gained.

There is a reason why I met Jake, loved Jake and lost Jake. I can't say I'm glad I felt so much pain, but there was also that warm, tingling feeling inside my heart. It's necessary for me to love beyond my fears and trust beyond my doubts if I want to truly live my life. And yes, perhaps my tears may fall, but I will not.

I guess a teenager's biggest fear is a broken heart. Mine used to be, but not anymore. Jake was worth it. After all, it is the wounded heart that makes us all human in the end.

Meredith Wertz

Staring Back at Me

Resolve to be thyself, and know that he who finds himself, loses his misery.

Matthew Arnold

When I was fifteen years old, I packed as many of my personal belongings as I could fit into two small backpacks and headed for the easy life. My only goals were to avoid responsibility and have as much fun as possible.

It was the beginning of summer, and I was sitting in my bedroom at my mom's house. We got into an argument over the usual teenage stuff. I didn't want to abide by my mom's rules, and I was feeling frustrated that "nothing ever went my way." When I left my house that day, I left with a feeling of liberation. I had won the battle with my mom. I was now in charge of my life.

I didn't know exactly where I was going, but I figured anywhere was an improvement. I spent the next few months couch-surfing from friend's house to friend's house. I would stay at each place until I had worn out my welcome. In less than a year, no one wanted me at their house, and people were starting to talk. See, I had a little secret, or what I thought was a secret. I had been using drugs quite heavily and supporting myself by stealing and selling my friends' material possessions.

I was a sixteen-year-old with no friends, no home, no self-esteem and no self-respect. I was sleeping in bank-machine booths and cardboard dumpsters to stay warm and dry in the winter. I considered suicide. I was over-whelmed by the feelings of hopelessness and despair that I felt on a daily basis. I lost a lot of weight. I hardly ever slept because of the drugs. The longer I was awake, the more desperate I would get. It became a vicious cycle.

I remember vividly the night I ended up at my sister's house. It was the middle of winter, and I had been living in another city in a speed lab—an abandoned house with torn-up plywood floors littered with garbage, dirt and bugs. I hadn't slept for thirteen days. I went back to my hometown intending to do some laundry, then leave. I don't remember how I got there, but I ended up at my sister's house where I was asked to "please stay." I was so confused. I hadn't had anyone want me around for so long that I was suspicious. But it wasn't a difficult decision. Either I went back to the streets, or I had a warm place to stay for a night. She gave me her bed, and I fell asleep.

When I woke up, I looked around until I found my sister. I was kind of in a daze. "What time is it?" I asked her.

"It's 9:30 P.M.," my sister told me.

"Oh, okay, then I've only been asleep for a couple hours," I replied.

"Well, no, Ben. Actually, it's Thursday, and you got here on Sunday," she informed me. "You've been sleeping for four days."

My sister, knowing that something wasn't right, told me I could stay with her for as long as I wanted to. I unpacked all my clothes the next day. I stayed with her and her boyfriend for almost a year and continued to use drugs. Unfortunately, my problem progressed and got worse. I was using every day, and I hated the person I had become. I wrote in my journal that I had a problem and wasn't able to stop. Pain was the only emotion I ever felt. I had been stuffing my feelings down with drugs for so long that I didn't know what feelings were anymore. I wasn't afraid of anything anymore. I prayed that I would die. I was depressed, and I had no motivation, dignity or ambition left whatsoever.

One night I jumped as the phone rang. I picked it up, and my mom was on the other end. I was scared to talk to her. She said she knew I was having a hard time dealing with what my life had become, and she wanted to read me a poem called *Footprints in the Sand.*

Instead of using the words "the Lord" she used herself. She told me that she would always be there for me if I needed her and that she would "carry" me through the toughest times of my life if I would let her. I finally understood the madness I had created. I had shut her out for so long because of a stupid decision I had made on an impulse one day over a year ago. But with her love that day, she broke through my walls of insecurity and pain. I just sat there and cried. I finally knew that someone cared.

When I hung up the phone, I felt incredibly guilty for what I had done to myself and the pain I had caused others. I was completely overwhelmed. I didn't know what to do. I was happy one moment because my mom still loved me, yet absolutely terrified the next. Through the tears I saw a knife on the dresser in front of me. Crying hysterically, I picked it up, and a feeling of calm and release came over me.

I woke up in the hospital bandaged and surrounded by people—my mom, my sister, my friend Emily and the nurses. I spent another month in the hospital, only this time I made a conscious effort to get help for my drug addiction. I started going to a twelve-step fellowship and met some people like me who were getting clean but had a while to go before they could rebuild any kind of life. On their recommendation, I decided to move into a recovery house. I lived there for ten months and now live on my own. I am finishing high school and enjoying life.

A lot has changed for me. The biggest change is that I feel good about myself and what I'm doing, and I have lost the desire to use drugs. My self-esteem is growing, and I have a huge group of friends. I have a relationship with my mom again. We talk almost every day. I have a job and people who love me. I spent my nineteenth birthday clean, with my family and friends. Today I can finally look in the mirror and be grateful for the person I see staring back at me.

Ben Jenkins

My Light

You are the light in my darkness,
my shelter in a storm.
You give me strength when I am weak,
and your love to keep me warm.
When I was hurting, lost, abused,
it was then your faith that I had used.
When I was cold, depressed and lonely,
I stayed alive by your love only.
When I felt pushed or shunned away,
it was then your friendship made me stay.
When I was sick and felt like dying,
I knew you loved me by your crying.
I knew you loved me, knew you cared,
you did what no one else had dared.
You took the time to learn, to see,
just what I really am in me.
You listened to my thoughts and fears,
and helped me wipe away my tears.
You helped me learn, respect and love,
to pray to God my Lord above.
You're the light in my darkness, I hope you'll see,
I'll love you, Mom, for eternity.

Robyn Robertson

Promises Kept

What a man sows, that shall he and his relations reap.

Clarissa Graves

My father was not a sentimental man. I don't remember him ever "oohing" or "aahing" over anything I did as a child. Don't get me wrong; I knew that my dad loved me, but getting all mushy-eyed was not his thing. He showed me love in other ways.

I always believed that my parents had a good marriage, but just before I turned sixteen my belief was sorely tested. My father, who used to share in the chores around the house, gradually started becoming despondent. From the time he came home from his job at the factory to the time he went to bed, he hardly spoke a word to any of us. The strain on their relationship was obvious. However, I was not prepared for the day Mom told us kids that Dad had decided to leave. I was stunned. It was something I never thought possible. I went totally numb and pretended like it wasn't happening until it actually came time for him to leave.

The night before my dad left, I stayed up in my
a long time. I prayed and cried. I wrote him a long
told him how much I loved him and how much I
miss him. As I folded my letter, I stuck in a picture of me
with a saying I had heard: "Anyone can be a father, but it
takes someone special to be a daddy." Early the next
morning, before my dad left, I sneaked out to his car and
slipped my letter into one of his bags.

Two weeks went by with hardly a word from him. Then
one afternoon I came home from school to find my mom
sitting at the dining-room table. I could see she had been
crying. She told me Dad had been over and that they had
talked for a long time. They decided there were things
they were willing to change—and they decided their marriage was worth saving. Then she looked at me.

"Kristi, Dad told me you wrote him a letter. Can I ask
what you wrote to him?" I mumbled a few words and
shrugged. Mom continued, "Well, he said that when he
read your letter, it made him cry. It meant a lot to him. I've
hardly ever seen your dad cry. After he read your letter, he
called to ask if he could come over to talk. Whatever you
said really made a difference to him."

A few days later my dad was back, this time to stay. We
never talked about the letter.

Over the next sixteen years, my siblings and I wit-
nessed one of the truly "great" marriages. Their love grew
stronger every day, and my heart swelled with pride as I
saw them grow closer together. When Mom and Dad
received news that his heart was rapidly deteriorating,
they were hand-in-hand throughout the ordeal.

After Dad's death, we had the unpleasant task of going
through his things. I opted to run errands so I wouldn't
have to be there while most of his things were divided and
boxed up. When I got back my brother said, "Kristi, Mom
said to give this to you. She said you would know what it

meant." My brother was holding the picture I had given Dad that day. My unsentimental dad, who never let his emotions get the best of him, my dad, who almost never outwardly showed his love for me, had kept the one thing that meant so much to both of us. I sat down and the tears began to flow as I realized what I had meant to him. Mom told me Dad had kept both the picture and the letter his whole life.

I have a box in my house that I call the "Dad Box." In it are things that remind me of my dad. I pull that picture out every once in a while and remember. I remember a promise made many years ago between a young man and his bride on their wedding day, and I remember the unspoken promise made between a father and his daughter—a promise kept.

Kristi Powers

Learning to Love

*Woe to the man whose heart has not learned
while young to hope, to love—and to put its trust
in life.*

Joseph Conrad

Trissa came up to me a few minutes before math class. "Hey, Richie, you know about cars," she said. "Mine's making a funny noise. Could you take a look at it?"

"Sure," I said, and then another girl named Arielle spoke up.

"Can I come watch?" she asked. "I want to learn how to fix cars, too."

A year ago I didn't even know what a distributor cap was. But nowadays my friends come to me with their car problems. They think I'm some kind of expert, but my new dad, Roger—he's the real expert. He taught me everything I know about engines and transmissions. But Roger also taught me more important stuff—about life and love, and what it truly means to become a man.

My real dad left when I was just a baby, and for fifteen

years it was just my mom and me. When the other guys played football with their dads I could only watch. And it was a little embarrassing going on fishing trips when my mom was the only woman there. But I convinced myself it didn't really matter. After all, how could I miss having a dad when I'd never had a dad to lose?

I was happy when we moved from Brooklyn to Nyack, New York, where my mom works for Sears. There was a lot more room to ride bikes and play ball, and at school there were coaches who taught me how to swing a bat and catch a pass—you know, the sort of things your dad's supposed to teach you.

I made a lot of new friends in Nyack, and my mom even started dating. Some of the guys were okay; others I thought were total jerks. But the night Mom and I met Roger at a New Year's Eve party, I didn't know what to think.

Roger was six feet, three inches tall and 250 pounds, with long hair and a beard. He was loud and a little hard of hearing, and his forearms were as big around as my thighs.

"Nice to meet you," Roger boomed when somebody introduced us. When he shook my hand it disappeared inside his huge paw, callused and scarred from years of construction work and working in the boiler room of a navy ship during the Vietnam War.

I thought Roger was one scary dude, but on the drive home when we talked about him, Mom got sort of dreamy. "He's actually very gentle," she said, and told me how sensitive Roger had seemed when he talked about his two sons who had drowned seventeen years before in a canoeing accident.

I still thought Roger was a little freaky, but a few nights later when he called I tried not to make a face as I handed Mom the phone. They talked for hours, and a few nights after that Roger took Mom to dinner. I didn't know whether to feel happy for her or worried she'd maybe flipped her lid.

Then one night Roger was sitting in our living room waiting for Mom to get ready while I was talking to my grandparents on the phone. I told my grandma I loved her when I finished talking to her, but to my grandfather I just said good-bye.

Hanging up, I was surprised when Roger cleared his throat to speak—and even more surprised by what he said. "I know why you didn't tell your grandfather you love him," he began. "It's because he's a guy, and you were embarrassed to tell him how you feel."

Roger talked some about his sons who had drowned. "Not a day passes when I don't wish I'd said 'I love you' to them even more than I did. 'I love you' isn't just something you say to women," he said. Now I was really confused because here was this giant tough guy with tears rolling down his cheeks.

I still remember the first time Mom and I visited Roger's house. The place overflowed with old newspapers and magazines, and everywhere you turned there were broken toasters and televisions Roger had always meant to fix. Then we went out to the garage—and wow!

Ever since I was little I've loved taking things apart to see how they work. Radios, my Ghostbusters game—I could take them apart fine, but there were always parts left over when I tried to put them back together. And the only tools I ever had were the screwdrivers and pliers from the kitchen drawer.

But Roger's garage was one big workshop full of tools I'd never even seen before.

For the next hour Roger showed me reciprocating saws, ratchets and about a thousand other tools. "Maybe one day we can work on a project together," he said, and I forced myself not to smile because what if he never did? What if Roger was just pretending to like me to impress my mom?

I guess you could say Roger swept my mom off her feet, because it wasn't long before we were packing our things to move into his house. Roger and I spent days hauling junk to the dump in his pickup. We also refinished the floors.

A few weeks later Roger taught me how to work a stick shift driving back and forth in the driveway. Then we went to the Department of Motor Vehicles to get my learner's permit.

Another day Roger brought home an old Ford Escort that barely ran. "We'll fix her up together, and then you'll have something to drive," he said. This time I didn't even try to hide my smile.

When we discovered the Escort's transmission was shot, Roger bought a used transmission from the junk-yard, and we jacked up the car and swapped it out with the old one. It was hard work, especially for a tall, skinny kid like me. But one night Mom gripped my forearm and smiled. "You're putting on muscle," she said.

"I know," I said proudly, and I owed it all to Roger.

Even after we got it running, Roger and I spent hours tinkering with my car, and we did a lot of talking while we worked. Roger told me about when he was my age and he and his dog Silus used to sit beside the tracks for hours watching the trains roll by, and how he'd worked at a gas station for free just so he could learn to fix cars.

Roger also talked about some of the many kids he'd taken into his home over the years—abused kids, kids strung out on drugs, even a few who had spent time in jail. Roger helped these guys through some pretty tough times, and many of them have grown up to become suc-cessful businessmen, policemen and firemen. They still come by with their wives and families to thank him.

These days our house is full of tiny parts from a piano Roger and I are rebuilding because we both want to know what makes it work. We also love going for long drives through the country, stopping at farms to check out the animals while we talk about life. Sometimes we talk about girls and sex and stuff like that, but after hearing stories about the kids Roger helped he didn't have to warn me about abusing drugs and alcohol. I don't want to screw up my life or wind up in prison. I want to grow up to be hard-working, honest and caring—just like Roger.

Besides my mom, Roger is the only person I know who will always be there for me, no matter what. Thanks to Roger I've grown tougher on the outside, but inside I know it's okay to care about people and tell them so.

Last Father's Day I wrote Roger a letter telling him how much he'd changed my life. "I never had a dad until I was a teenager, but now I have the greatest dad in the world," I wrote. "You've taken me places I never would have gone, both out in the world and inside myself, and your 'I love yous' are the most reassuring and wonderful words I've ever heard in my life."

Bernard "Richie" Thomassen
As told to Heather Black

My Superhero

To love another person is to see the face of God.
Victor Hugo

Everyone has a hero—someone he admires, who has had an impact on his life. My brother, John, is my hero. He is the most compassionate, sweet and funny person I have ever met. John is also mentally retarded and has a developmental disability known as autism.

I used to be ashamed of John when I was little. When he first started talking, he had a hard time with pronunciation and understanding the meaning of words. He called me May-Me for most of my childhood because he could not pronounce Amy. As John grew older, his language ability gradually increased. I went from May-Me to Amy, and hammer burgers became hamburgers.

Now I rather enjoy John's mispronunciations and mixing of phrases. For example, instead of "eagle-eyes," John called himself "four-eyes" once, and rather than getting something "off his chest," he prefers to get things "over his back." Instead of people getting their ears boxed, John thinks people get books put on their ears.

When I was younger, I was embarrassed by John. He used to gallop around in stores talking to himself, flicking his ears and putting his hands in his mouth. He had a hard time swallowing and would have drool running down his face. John was very loud, and it seemed to me that he would always find the quietest moments to talk.

All I ever wanted was a normal brother. I would look at other brothers and sisters, see their relationships and turn green with envy. Why did my brother have to be so different? I was very self-conscious of what people thought. I felt as if the entire world was laughing at me because of the way John was acting. I was outraged at times that I could not have a normal brother.

John has changed significantly over the past eighteen years. As he grew older, he became social and adopted an upbeat and positive attitude. John began to see things for what they really are.

Most people feel sorry for John, and they feel as if they should be the one helping him. John, however, does not even see that he has a problem, only that there are problems out there that people need help with, and he wants to help. If my mentally handicapped brother can have so many problems of his own, overcome these problems as if they are nothing and want to help others, then surely I can overcome obstacles of my own.

The siblings of an autistic child can have many reactions to the amount of attention the autistic child receives. Some feel as if they are not receiving enough attention and may become superachievers to get their share. I hate to admit it, but I definitely fall into this category. I feel the need to excel in everything I do. I cannot help but think that this comes from having a disabled brother. I do not feel it comes so much from the need for attention, but instead from the need to do it because John cannot. I need to seize every opportunity I can because I know some people will never have that opportunity. John has taught me to do as much as I can with what I have.

The name John means "gift from God." No one knows for sure what causes autism, and there is no cure. I do not, however, ask God anymore why he did this to John. Instead, I thank him for making John the way he did. As I grow older, I'm no longer ashamed of my brother; instead, I am ashamed that I used to be. There is no one I would rather walk through a store with, no one I would rather have a "quiet" conversation with in the midst of a quiet restaurant. I beam with pride when someone tells me they love my brother, because I know I am truly blessed to have John in my life to keep me real and remind me of what is important. John has taught me to live life, to love life and, no matter what, that life goes on. So maybe John is no Clark Kent, but he is definitely a superhero and a gift from God.

Amy Rene Byrne

Safe at Last

I'm so afraid.
Afraid that people might see
Who I really am.
I try to hide it:
Outside I'm calm, cool, collected.
But inside I'm crumbling
Into a million pieces.
I can't hide it forever;
Sometimes the mask slips off
And I'm exposed and vulnerable.
I feel so naked
And everyone is looking at me.
They can see right through me.
But I put my mask back on
And I'm safe behind it.
Nothing can happen to me there.
Safe.
But the fear comes back again
Just like it always does.
Then I'm crying out again,
Crying for help inside.

The mask comes off again.
That's when I feel him
Holding my hand.
The voice says,
"Do not fear, my child,
For I love you exactly as you are
And I will always be with you."
Suddenly a peace comes over me
And I'm not afraid anymore
Because I know he loves me
Just the way I am.

Bethany Schwartz

Missing the Dance

In the sweetness of friendship let there be laugh-
ter and sharing of pleasures.

Kahlil Gibran

I couldn't believe he was asking me. My two best friends
had gotten dates weeks ago, so I had given up hope of anyone asking me to the winter dance. Rick was the coolest
guy in the senior class! And he wanted to go with me?

"Are you serious?"

"I've already taken care of the tickets, and my parents
will let me use their car," he assured me.

My mouth worded, "Yes," as my heart leaped with joy. I
had never been to a formal dance before, and now was my
chance. This would be the best night of my life.

The moment I got home I told my mom about Rick's
invitation. Immediately, she took me shopping to find the
perfect dress. We decided on how to fix my hair and what
color nail polish to wear.

Before I knew it, days had passed. I couldn't sleep at all.
Butterflies fluttered in my stomach, and my head was

throbbing. Friday morning I woke up, and the whole world seemed to spin. I tried to lift my head off the pillow, but I couldn't move.

"Honey, you're going to be late for school. Are you okay?" My mom came into the bedroom. Her hand went to my forehead. "Oh, no! You've got a fever."

I didn't feel hot; I felt cold, very cold.

My mother helped me dress and drove me to the doctor. I had been there only a few minutes before my doctor called an ambulance. I couldn't understand what he was telling me. All I could hear was a muffled, "One-hundred-four-degree fever."

The hospital looked so blindingly bright as a nurse stuck two IVs in my arm. I didn't remember seeing her come into my room, only the blanket being thrown on top of me. "Cold, very cold," I responded.

"It's filled with ice," she explained. "You have a bad infection. Your doctor ordered fluids and antibiotics for you. Just rest."

I closed my eyes.

It seemed only a few minutes later when I heard my doctor's voice. "Good morning. I'm glad you slept through the night. Luckily, we've brought your temperature down. You are one special girl. You have a very serious infection, but it seems we have it under control."

"Mom?" I gasped. "Dad?"

"We're right here." My mother grabbed my hand.

I looked up at them.

"Did I miss the dance?"

My mom smiled. "I called Rick. I got his number out of your address book and let him know that you were in the hospital."

"Oh, no," I cried.

"There will be other dances," said my doctor. "Be thankful you'll be alive to see them."

Days passed, and I got increasingly stronger and no longer had a fever. The medical staff discovered that I had developed a bad strep infection, which my doctor treated with antibiotics.

I hadn't heard from Rick at all. That bothered me. I worried that he was angry. Not only had I missed the dance, but I had let him down. Who could blame him if he never spoke to me again?

The same nurse who had given me my IVs came into my room holding a hospital robe. "Put this on," she said.

"Why? Aren't I going home today? I have a gown on already."

She just smiled and left, shutting the door behind her. I didn't feel like putting on the robe, but I did what she asked. Maybe there was another X ray or test my doctor needed before I could be released.

Suddenly, the door swung open. Standing before me were my parents holding balloons and a CD player, my two best friends in formals, and their dates and Rick in tuxedos.

"Would you care for a dance?" Rick asked. "Just because you missed the winter dance doesn't mean we can't have our own right here, right now."

Tears came to my eyes. "Sure," I stammered.

The nurse closed the curtains and left only the bathroom light on. My friends coupled together as Rick wrapped his arms around me and began to sway to the music.

"I'm so glad you're okay," he said. "I called your parents every night to check up on you."

"They didn't tell me." I pulled at my hair so it would look brushed.

"Don't worry," he smiled. "You look beautiful."

My friends and I danced for what seemed like hours. We didn't mind the people watching from the hall or my parents dancing beside us. My hospital robe was less than formal, but I didn't care. When the CD was over, Rick helped me into a wheelchair and took me downstairs to his parents' car, which was waiting to take me home.

I will never forget that afternoon for as long as I live. I didn't have my hair done or a pretty dress on, but I felt truly beautiful and truly loved.

Michele "Screech" Campanelli

7

ANGELS AMONG US

*F*or *he shall give his angels charge over thee to
keep thee in all thy ways.*

Psalms 91:11

Angels Among Us

There are things in life
That will make you cry,
And it's times like these
When you barely get by.

There are people in life
Who will make it hard,
There are times when you'll feel
Like you're on your guard.

But up in the sky,
The stars shine bright,
Over your sorrows
And all through the night.

Upon those stars,
The angels watch,
And guide us through
Life's toughest parts.

They make us laugh
And dry our tears,
They release our anger
And calm our fears.

There are angels among us
When you're feeling blue,
And when you feel alone,
They come to you.

They pick you up
And hold your hand,
They walk with you,
They understand.

So the sadder you get
And the worse you feel,
Always remember,
Angels are here.

Kerri Knipper

He Sees

Recently in church, the sermon was about Jesus' challenge to his people: "Do you see what I see?" The pastor spoke about using the eyes of Jesus to identify the needs of a person, rather than focusing on outward appearance only.

When I was growing up, I often felt different. My parents were missionaries, and we moved between Austria, Turkey, Germany and our home base in Illinois more than eleven times. I attended twelve different schools before college. After depositing me in Indiana at a small Christian university, my parents were on their way back to Germany for the next four years. I was emotionally exhausted.

I wasn't close to God, although I had had some spiritual experiences that assured me of my connection with God. I felt tired by the time I started college. I was tired of starting over all the time, tired of always being told what to do and tired of years of never feeling rooted in a place I could call home. I spent a lot of time in my dorm room, consumed by increasingly depressed thoughts.

As a true missionary kid, at first I tried to make friends with people. But I longed for one true friend I could trust.

Finally, I gave up and kept to my room. I felt unloved and deserted.

I was shocked by how dark my thoughts had become. I actually entertained thoughts of wondering how many pills it would take to get me out of the terrible spot I was in. I became physically run down and developed a terrible cold, which was what drove me out of my room to the campus clinic.

While I was waiting my turn to see the doctor, Mike approached me. The only contact I'd had with Mike was when he had helped my roommate's father set up loft beds for my roommate and me. I had to actually concentrate on remembering his name as he approached. He sat down beside me. Looking vaguely uncomfortable, he said, "When you're done with the doctor, I'd like to speak with you. Will you have a minute?"

I agreed without much enthusiasm. There was a school banquet coming up, and I distractedly thought he looked uncomfortable because he was going to ask me to attend the banquet with him. I spent the entire time being examined by the doctor, dreading the prospect of being asked to go to an event I had no desire of attending with someone I barely knew. When I was finished, Mike reappeared. We stood outside the clinic, and the awkwardness was almost palpable.

He looked at me and said, "I have something to tell you, and I feel a little weird about saying this, but if you could bear with me until I'm finished ... I really think God wants me to tell you this."

There was an uncomfortable pause as he waited for my permission to go on. I must have nodded some sort of assent, thinking this was easily one of the weirdest ways anyone had ever asked me out on a date. What came next was very much unexpected.

He told me, "I've been praying for you. God has really

put your name on my heart. He's been guiding me to tell you he knows you've been having suicidal thoughts. I know this sounds crazy, but he wanted me to tell you that you are not alone, and he loves you."

I suddenly felt exposed. I didn't even know this guy, and here he was telling me not to end my life. Who did he think he was? What gave him the right to talk to me like I had lost my mind? I wasn't crazy, just tired of feeling like nobody understood me.

Then I took a deep breath and tried to open my heart to what was happening. From a place of calm, I suddenly realized Mike was God's messenger. God understood! Mike had taken a huge personal risk approaching me, a person he didn't even know, with a message he didn't really understand. I gathered myself together enough to thank him and ask him to keep praying because I needed it, then I made my escape back to my room.

As I sat on my bed and examined the conversation, I was overcome by the amazing fact that God knew where I was and had used one of his servants to deliver hope. I felt warmed and encouraged. Although I didn't immediately snap out of my depression, I felt comfort in the realization that God knew how badly I was hurting.

I have been through down times since, but I've realized that through all of the inevitable ups and downs of life, God reaches out to individuals when they need him. I remember that encounter often, and I feel incredibly blessed to have been the recipient of such a message of love. The world is a better place because of people like Mike—people willing to see others through the eyes of Jesus.

Kristina J. Adams

The Days We Prayed

It must be recess in heaven if St. Peter is letting his angels out.
Zora Neale Hurston

I was thirty-five years old and an hour and a half into my new teaching career when I saw Jason at the opposite end of the hallway. He was the reason I almost didn't take the job. Then later, a hundred times when I wanted to quit, he was the reason I didn't.

Jason was a special-needs student, thirteen years old and pretty much confined to a wheelchair since birth. As the school's newest special-education teacher, it would be my job to teach Jason and attend to his personal needs. He had medicines that would have to be administered and diapers that would need to be changed twice a day—odd tasks for a man who had made a habit of fleeing his own kids at medicine and diaper-changing time.

My educational background was in business, but there had been no positions available in that area. To take the job meant I would have to return to school during summers and evenings in order to obtain the necessary certification. Because my own kids attended this school system, I wanted very much to be a part of it, and special education was the only position available.

I expected an angry child, resentful of what life had delivered, and as I watched him approach, I had to admit that Jason had every right to be. His condition was called spina bifida, a congenital defect of the vertebrae. He had already undergone a dozen surgeries, and his family anticipated more. He was being cared for full-time by elderly grandparents.

His prognosis, too, was poor. Only a season before I had attended the school's sixth-grade graduation. At that ceremony, his grandmother had invited the entire family, and had ordered balloons and flowers for the event. She wanted the celebration to be special for Jason because, as she later explained, it might be the only graduation he would ever see.

Yet if Jason was embittered, I saw no sign of it that day. As he approached slowly and steadily, he must have realized who I was and held out both arms in greeting. "Welcome, friend. It's good to see you!"

Though it took us awhile to adjust—Jason as a new junior-high student and I as a new teacher—we eventually came to terms. More than a student, Jason became a friend. Later, Jason became like a son.

During our times together, Jason shared his heart. He told me he had attended church for as long as he could remember. A couple of years before he had turned his life over to Jesus, and someday he hoped to become a preacher. Though Jason never made it into the ministry, I believe he helped me grow as a Christian and as a teacher.

I remember one time in particular, when his eighty-year-old grandfather had become ill, Jason asked me to pray with him. As a first-year teacher and not tremendously secure with my own future, I was reluctant. Tactfully, I brushed away the suggestion, explaining that the government had guidelines and regulations about teachers and students praying together on school grounds.

Jason, as always, seemed to understand.

Two hours later, though, when Jason was in his band class, God spoke to me—not in an audible voice, but rather with a feeling of deep remorse that weighed heavily on my heart. It is a sad world indeed, I came to realize, when a public-school teacher is so wrapped up in the system that he is afraid to pray with a frightened child. I dropped what I was doing and went among the tubas and clarinets to find my friend. I wheeled him back to the nurse's station, and there in the quiet of the room, Jason and I prayed for his grandfather.

Shortly thereafter, Jason's grandfather began his recovery. Many times after that, Jason and I prayed together. I shared with Jason that I often prayed silently in my classroom, and Jason suggested a way that he and I could pray silently together. He would lay his pencils (he always had at least two) on his desk in the form of a cross as a signal to me that he was praying. Silently then, from wherever I was in the room, I would join him.

Once, when I was having a bad day, Jason's friend Delbert came to class without a pencil. Jason and Delbert knew what a stickler I was for bringing necessary materials to class, and Jason would often secretly loan things to Delbert. I noticed (and though I was annoyed, said nothing) as Jason slipped a pencil to his friend.

Later, I gave a written assignment and was surprised when Jason wheeled up to my desk with tears welling in his eyes. "I don't have my pencil," he said, and immediately I remembered Delbert.

"Jason," I said, almost in a shout. "If you didn't keep giving your things to Delbert, you'd have a pencil, wouldn't you?" Then as I looked up, I noticed a pencil in his shirt pocket. All the more annoyed that the disruption had been entirely unnecessary, I pulled out the pencil and held it in front of him. "Jason, here's your pencil."

A tear rolled down his cheek. "That's the pencil I *write* with," he explained. "It's the pencil I *pray* with that I don't have."

From that moment forward, I made a point to have lots of spare materials on hand. Sometimes my students come to school in the winter with no socks on their feet or coats on their backs. A pencil, at times, seems like a small thing.

It was late last year, on the Thursday before he went in for a scheduled heart surgery, that Jason (now an eleventh-grader) and I prayed for what would be the last time. He hugged me as he left that day and, as I returned to the classroom to gather my belongings for the trip home, I saw the desk where he sat and the two pencils he had left behind.

When I think of Jason now, I remember perhaps the most remarkable young man I have ever known, yet I have a hard time becoming sad for him, because I know he was not afraid.

And I know that I will see him again one day, only this time without the chair that bound him as a child. In my mind, I see him there in the distance, standing with a friend, the same friend who once answered his prayers and who, from heaven, watched over Jason as he toiled and struggled with life's situations below. The struggles now are gone, but the happy smiles remain, and with laughing eyes and open arms he makes his way toward me.

"Welcome, friend. It's good to see you!"

Hugh T. Chapman

Reprinted by permission of Randy Glasbergen.

I Just Wanna Be a Sheep

Teaching is the greatest act of optimism.

Colleen Wilcox

I stood at the head of the long table, watching helplessly as the five young boys in my class fought over chairs, exchanged bops on the head and tried to balance crayons on the tips of their noses.

"Hey, scoot over. I'm sitting there."

"I was here first."

"Both of you move. That's *my* seat."

"I don't see your name on it."

"Toss me that crayon!"

"This is the song that doesn't end . . . ."

"Aw, man! Tyler, no one likes that song!"

"I got a pet snake at home. He eats mice. Swallows 'em whole!"

"My dog eats grass and barfs on the carpet."

"And they will keep on singing it forever, just because. . . ."

"Hey, what are you guys doing in my chair?"

"It's my chair!"

"Is not."

"Is too!"

"Hey, you! Teacher person, girl in charge! Tell them to get out of my seat, will ya!"

I closed my eyes and took several slow, deep breaths. It was only the first ten minutes of the first day of Vacation Bible School, and I already felt like I had completely lost control.

Of course, that would've required me to *have* control in the first place.

I glanced over at Jaimi, my friend and fellow "teacher person, girl in charge" of our church's Vacation Bible School primary class. Jaimi raised her eyebrows and gave me a look that said, "How did we get ourselves into this?"

I shrugged helplessly. A month ago it had seemed like a great idea to volunteer to teach this class. Now I wasn't so sure. Did we really expect five energetic seven-to-nine-year-old boys to listen to a couple of teenage girls?

I turned back to the table just in time to catch one of the boys plopping himself down in a chair, right on top of his best friend. "I told you to get out of my seat," he said. The other boy squealed, flailing his arms and legs like an over-turned beetle.

"Get off of him, Brian!" I commanded, referring to the kid's nametag, which he had so elegantly stuck to his forehead.

"It's okay," came the muffled voice of the boy who was being squashed into a pancake. I remembered reading the name Jordan on his tag, moments before he was flattened. "It's actually kind of fun," Jordan said.

"Get off, anyway," I replied. Brian reluctantly slid into another chair. "Now everyone grab a seat." Brian jumped back up and hoisted his chair high into the air.

"I grabbed it," he announced proudly. "Now what do I do with it?"

When Jaimi and I finally managed to get the class somewhat settled down, I got out my trusty *VBS Teacher's Guide* to find out what came first on our agenda.

"Okay," I said cheerfully, clapping my hands together. "Now we're going to play a game where we all learn each other's names."

My announcement was received with loud moans and groans.

"That's baby stuff," said Brian.

"Yeah, we're not babies!" another kid piped up.

"That junk's for the kindergarten class," said Jordan.

"Kindergarten baby, stick your head in gravy!" Tyler sang.

I breathed a heavy sigh. This was going to be a long week.

The issue of whether an activity was too "babyish" came up often over the next few days. *It can't be easy*, I realized, *being stuck in the middle like these kids are.* The primary class was too young to do some of the cool stuff that the older ones got to do, yet too old to be entertained with puppet shows and sing-alongs. I soon realized that if I wanted to keep these boys interested, I needed to learn to improvise.

"This story's boring," Brian announced one day during lesson study. The other boys heartily agreed.

"We already know about Noah's ark."

"I have this book at home. I've seen all the pictures a million times."

"It's a baby story. I want to hear about Samson again, and how they gouged his eyeballs out!"

"Yeah, are there any more stories where they gouge out people's eyeballs?"

"No eyeball gouging!" I exclaimed. "Come on, you guys! Today's story is about Noah."

"Boring!" Brian declared.

I thought fast. "Okay," I said, "I'm sure you all know this story inside and out, so why don't you tell it to us?"

I could see another "boring" about to explode from

Brian's lips, so I quickly added, "How about you guys act it out? You can pretend to be Noah and his sons and all the animals."

"Cool! I want to be a pig!"

"What if I want to be the pig?"

"You can be the girl pig."

"Look, I'm a dog! Woof, woof, woof!"

"I'm a lion! Roar!"

"Hey," Jordan breathed in almost a whisper, "can I be God?"

It was probably the most original reenactment of Noah's ark that had ever been performed, yet we managed to get through it just like we got through everything else—with tons of smiles and plenty of laughter.

One of the most important lessons I learned that week about dealing with kids was that you need to be able to kick back and be a kid yourself sometimes. So every day Jaimi and I would join our class outside for a rousing game of tag or hide-and-seek. We always had fun, and it was a great way to work off energy.

Of course, some of us had a lot more energy than others.

"Brian, get out of the neighbor's flower bed!" I hollered one day when our little "Mr. Rambunctious" had trampled through the next-door neighbor's daffodils for the third time in twenty minutes.

"No, Brian, you cannot hide in other people's cars," I informed him during hide-and-seek. "And you definitely can't drive them!"

Brian was our troublemaker, all right, but in a way I kind of enjoyed because he kept me on my toes. The other boys looked up to him and followed his lead, which often led us all into some very interesting situations.

At the end of Vacation Bible School, there was going to be a program for all the parents, during which each class would perform a song. To prove to our boys that I didn't think they were babies, I brought in a split-track CD of kids' Christian songs and let them choose for themselves the one they wanted to do.

"I like the sheep song," Brian spoke up.

I played "I Just Wanna Be a Sheep" again for everyone to hear. It was a fun, upbeat song, but it had a lot of verses, and I wondered how the boys would ever learn it in time.

Over the next few days, Jaimi and I worked those kids like little soldiers, making them practice every spare second. But, as with most activities, they were always much more interested in running around and causing trouble than in doing what they were supposed to.

The morning before the program the boys still hadn't learned the song very well, and they were thoroughly sick of practicing. In a desperate attempt to lift their spirits, I did what any good teacher would do under such circumstances: I bribed them.

"If you guys do well tonight, I'll bring you all presents, okay? Just try and sing loud enough for people to hear you." I started the music up once more.

"I just wanna be a sheep, baa baa baa baa!" The boys sang decently for about half the song, but even the prospect of a surprise wasn't encouraging them as much as I'd hoped.

As the kids lay sprawled out across the floor, taking a break from practicing, I tried to explain to them what it meant to be a sheep: how God is our shepherd and how we should always follow Him. I had just about given up all hope of them ever learning, much less understanding the song, when the most amazing thing happened.

Brian, the boy who had from the very first day caused us the most trouble, suddenly started singing, by himself, without the music. And, miracle of miracles, the other boys joined in. They sang loud and clear, without messing up or goofing around. They sat right there on the floor and sang the entire song while I held my breath.

When they were finished, I practically exploded.

"That was excellent!" I exclaimed. "If you guys sing half that good tonight, you'll blow everyone away!"

And that's exactly what they did. Those boys sang "I Just Wanna Be a Sheep" by Brian M. Howard, with all the energy and enthusiasm they had shown throughout the week. And as I sat in the church pew listening, I was sure that I had never been prouder in my entire life. I also felt a little like how God must feel toward His sheep. Sometimes they follow Him; sometimes they don't. Sometimes they get into trouble; sometimes they make Him laugh. But no matter what, He always loves them.

I felt blessed to have had the chance to be a sort of shepherd to those boys, even for just one week, and I had a new respect for the difficult job God has to do all the time. I know I could never handle it. I'm happy just being one of His sheep.

Christina Marie Dotson

Adventures in Children's Story Time

Batman and Robin Forever

Angels can fly because they take themselves lightly.

G. K. Chesterton

On that first day in late June, the sun was shining bright on the dew-stained grass. I stood with the other counselors prepared to meet the children whom I had read so much about. Not knowing what to expect, a small boy with brown hair and dark eyes approached me. "Me, Andrew," he exclaimed excitedly. "In Group Two with you." His speech was choppy and hard to understand, but the look on his face made me smile. Kneeling down, Andrew unzipped his backpack and took out a crumpled piece of paper. "For you," he said, tossing the paper at me. "Friends forever like Batman and Robin," I read out loud. Flashing me a big, goofy grin, Andrew stood up, kissed me on the cheek and ran off to play with the other children.

Batman and Robin—words I won't ever forget. Not just because little Andrew used them to explain how he felt, but because they signify all the relationships that I have ever experienced. Love, commitment, trust and, at times, hardship—all wrapped up in the words of a mentally challenged eight-year-old boy. Andrew's perception of life, combined with my own, created bonds of friendship that will live forever in my heart.

Whenever I connect with someone and find their soul, I remember that warm day in June. I remember Andrew and the words he spoke that explained my life. Many people believed that Andrew didn't really know what he was saying. The other counselors said he was just thinking about his favorite action figures and didn't know the significance of his words. On the last day of camp, Andrew came to me in tears. He told me he was afraid that Batman and Robin weren't going to see each other anymore. When I asked him if they could still be friends, Andrew dried his tears and grabbed his backpack. He took out a piece of paper and a pencil and sat down on the grass.

Slowly, he maneuvered his pencil to form what his mind kept repeating over and over again. Handing me the paper, he looked up at me with his tear-stained face.

"Batman and Robin Forever," is what he had written.

Elizabeth Hannibal

My Lollipop

Ice. Snow. Cold. It was the lovely month of February, when everyone was sick of the snow, and spring still felt light-years away. The cold air on windows during February, however, always did make for good pictures in the stream of my breath.

As I drew a heart on the window, something outside caught my eye. It was a girl. She wore designer clothes and had a pretty face. She is the type who wakes up at 5:30 to leave enough time to fix her makeup, even though school starts at 7:25. She was surrounded by a group of her friends, all of them chatting and laughing as they left the school. I envied her. Not because she was beautiful or because she had enough friends to last her a lifetime. I envied her because it seemed as if she knew exactly who she was and where she wanted to be. The arrival of a white Camry interrupted my thoughts. Her ride was there. She waved good-bye to her clique as she climbed into the front seat, and the car door slammed.

The car door brought my mind back to the night before. It sounded just like my bedroom door had after I slammed it in an effort to escape from my mother's angry voice. Her screams followed me to my room, however, and somehow found a way to penetrate my door. They will remain with me for years to come.

Ten minutes before, I had pushed my four-year-old brother out of my path to reach something. "Get out of my way," I said.

"No!" replied my brother. He has a way of constantly being directly in the way of something I need, and it does no good to reason with him. So instead of wasting my time and energy that night, I just moved him out of the way. This annoyed my mother. She started yelling about how terrible I was with children. Now, in order to understand why this upset me so much, there is something you must know. Anyone who has discussed my career plans with me knows that I love kids. I not only plan on working with them in the future, but I work with them now as well, and I thoroughly enjoy myself. My mother knows this, yet she continued to scream herself hoarse. "You have the worst personality when it comes to children. You had better start changing your plans quick!" This stung. It was probably the worst thing she could have said to me.

I sighed as I managed to pull myself from the window. The room started to come back into focus. On one side, there were tables with chairs and a blackboard. The other side was more interesting and was separated into little kitchen areas. Spoons were set out on the counter, along with bowls and plastic molds. Chocolate would appear later, ready to be molded into candy.

As I examined the pictures carved into the plastic molds, Mrs. Festa came in with more supplies. She is the advisor of a club called Helping Little Hands. The club's mission is to help and plan activities for underprivileged children.

I heard another car door slam outside, but this time I was too busy to be looking out the window. Mrs. Festa and I had started to melt the chocolate. Within seconds of hearing the car door, eager feet could be heard pounding down the hallway. The children had arrived.

Every year, we invite the children to our club to make cookies or chocolate at holiday times. The children are always excited to come back and have memorized the rules by now. They all know to get an apron and to wash their hands before touching anything. After those things are completed, the children wait for instructions. (I have a sneaking suspicion even those have been memorized as well.)

We explained how to spoon the different-colored chocolates into the heart-shaped molds, and the kids jumped right into the project, even the youngest ones, too short to reach the counter. There were quite a few kids to lift that day.

Whenever I am with children, I do my best never to pick a favorite. However, there are always one or two kids I find especially interesting. On this day, there was a certain boy I was drawn to. He was ten, but his attitude and the aura of toughness he was trying to uphold told the story of a boy who had been hardened by the world and all the trouble it had caused him. His face looked much older than ten.

I especially noticed the lollipop he was making. Most of the children had finished with their projects. There wasn't much chocolate left. He took the remaining spoonfuls of all the different colors, so jumbled that a person could not see where one color started and the next ended.

Over two hours had passed. It was time for everyone to go. Each of the children was given a bag, and they all split the candy amongst themselves to take with them. The ten-year-old boy came back over to me after he had gotten his share of candy. He noticed my hands were empty. "Why didn't you take any?" he asked.

"I wanted to make sure there was enough for everyone else," I said.

"Oh," he replied, but I could see he didn't really accept my answer.

As everyone got ready to leave, I was occupied with buttoning coats and didn't see the boy staring at me. I got a hug from each of the smiling children as they slipped out the door.

"Terrible with children," my mother had said. As much as the previous night had made me angry, now her words saddened me. It dawned on me that my mother didn't just say that because she was angry. She said it because she really believed it was true. It made me sad that my own mother hadn't taken the time or energy to know anything about who I really am.

My ten-year-old friend was the last to go. By now, I had noticed the little tough guy looking at me. He came up to me again, this time slowly, looking around to make sure no one was watching.

"This is for you," he said, as he handed me a piece of candy. It was the last lollipop he had made, the heart-shaped one with all the different colors mixed together. I smiled as he motioned me downward with his finger. As I bent over, he whispered into my ear, "You're my favorite grown-up." For a second, his tough, hardened face broke into a wide, childish grin.

I kept that lollipop, that piece of chocolate made by a child's hands, for months afterward. With all its colors in disarray, the stick on it chipped and the ribbon frayed, that lollipop remains a special treasure. I may never know exactly who I am or where I'm supposed to be, but however insignificant it is to anyone else, I do know one thing: I am his favorite grown-up, and for now, that is all that matters.

Andrea Mendez

Thirty Cents Worth

Whispering voices and laughter fill the hallways of my school as I walk with my friend toward our next class. I resist the impulse to become yet another person using these few moments to judge others in order to make myself feel better. I repeat to myself, *Thirty cents,* as I continue to walk in silence, something I rarely do. My friend digs her elbow into my side and grumbles, "That's just gross. Why would anyone want blue hair? That's so nasty!" I think before my tongue springs into action. Ordinarily, I would just give the expected giggle and nod—but for some reason, I hesitate.

My thoughts turn back to the previous Sunday afternoon. After flying through the house grabbing and tossing things into my soccer bag, I discovered that I was out of Blister-Block Band-Aids, an essential for the next day's game. After some persuasion, I coaxed my mom into taking me to Walgreen's. She dropped me off and assured me she'd be right back. I rushed inside and snatched the goods.

There was a line at the register, as usual, and I waited my turn. I slowed down for a minute and examined the man in front of me. I was appalled.

He was old and reeked of gasoline and cigarettes. His hair was unkempt and reached below his shoulders. He wore a red vest matted in dust and jeans faded beyond recognition. His blue eyes were glassy and tired, and his dark mahogany face was etched with deep wrinkles carved by hard times.

He reached the counter and greeted the saleswoman with a nod. She averted her eyes as he pointed to the cigarettes behind the counter. She grabbed the carton he was pointing to and quickly rang him up. He grabbed the plastic bag and slowly ambled away.

I gave her four one-dollar bills and the Band-Aids as she nodded in agreement with my disgust. "Sorry," she said. "You're thirty cents short."

"Oh, no . . . I don't have thirty cents! My mom isn't here. . . . She'll be right back. Can I run out to the car real quick?" As I was pleading my case, the cashier was visibly annoyed by the delay I was causing. I could feel the blood rush to my face as the people behind me in line started looking at each other with the same judgmental eyes I had just shared with the cashier. Just as I was about to run out of the store without my Band-Aids, I got a strong whiff of cigarettes and gasoline.

A dirty hand with yellow fingernails placed four nickels and a dime on the counter. I was awestruck and at a loss for words. I quickly offered to pay him back.

"That's okay. It's only thirty cents," he said with a warm smile and a wink. The man I had just judged as a foul creature had done something amazingly kind.

Now when I start to judge somebody based on their looks, I stop and repeat "thirty cents" to myself as a reminder to look beyond appearances. When I do that, I see beauty in everyone I meet.

Trish E. Calvarese

The Prayer Cards

Angels are both God's messengers and God's message, witnesses to eternity in time, to the presence of the divine amidst the ordinary. Every moment of every day is riddled by their traces.
                                        F. Forrester Church

I had known my friend George's grandmother, Mrs. Teague, for years. I had always liked her, but I was surprised when the phone rang one day shortly before the beginning of my junior year in high school.

After a few polite remarks back and forth between us, she got down to the purpose of her call. "I wonder if you would like to do some work for me. For a while now, I have been unable to get out and go the way I used to. But I want to continue to do whatever I can to help people. A while back I began seeing to it that prayer cards were placed on each patient's hospital tray on Sunday morning at the hospital. Mary Debs has been typing those cards for me, but she will be going off to college, so I need to find someone else who can do the typing. I thought of you and wondered if you would be interested in doing it."

I was interested. I found the idea of making a little extra money (and it was only a little) inviting, but I also thought the project itself seemed like a worthy one.

"Yes, Mrs. Teague, I would be interested. What exactly would it involve?"

"Well, what I generally do is call on Saturday and give Mary Debs the prayer over the phone. She types the prayer on plain index cards and takes the cards to the hospital sometime later that day so the people in the kitchen can be sure they are on the trays the next morning. I call the hospital to see how many patients there are each Saturday so I will know how many cards to have you prepare from week to week. I can give you that number when I call to give you the prayer."

I know we talked about money, too, and how much she would pay me, but I can't even recall that amount now. I just know that it sounded reasonable to me, and I wanted to be part of this dear lady's ministry, so I gladly accepted the assignment and began a job that lasted for two years.

True to her word, Mrs. Teague would call each Saturday with a patient count and a prayer, a different one each week. And the prayers were not prayers she was getting from some book, even though that would have been fine. Rather, they were prayers that came from her own heart as she looked at the list of patients and tried to compose a brief prayer that would speak to those people's needs. The prayers were never long, but they were always meaningful. I would give anything now if I had had the foresight to keep a copy of each prayer I typed. But young people generally don't hold on to those kinds of things, and being the typical teen that I was, I didn't keep any.

What I have kept, though, is the memory of those phone calls and the sound of Mrs. Teague's voice as she would begin each week's conversation with, "Hello, Mary. This is

Mrs. Teague. How are you?" And we would visit briefly—
a sixteen-year-old girl and a seventy-four-year-old grandmother. This precious woman would tell me how much
she wished she was able to go and visit the sick like she
used to, but that she had realized one thing she could still
do was pray. This prayer ministry was her way of continuing to serve the Lord she loved. She believed in the power
of prayer and was convinced that if she were faithful in
doing what she still could, God would take care of His
part. After the visiting part of our conversation, which was
usually very brief, she would say, "Our prayer for this
week will be . . ." And then she would read a beautiful,
simple prayer that she had thought about all week.

When she had completed her dictation, I would read
the prayer back to her, be sure I knew the number of
patients to prepare for and bid her farewell until next Saturday. It was our weekly ritual.

Because my Saturdays were often crazy, I usually didn't
get to sit down and type the cards right after the call. More
often than not, I typed them after I got home from whatever I was doing on Saturday night and took them to the
hospital kitchen in plenty of time for Sunday breakfast.
There were nights when it was 2:30 A.M. when I delivered
the prayers, but they were always there on time.

Today, this job would be quite different. I'd sit down at
a computer, type a prayer and print as many copies of it as
I needed. But in those days, I typed each card on a manual
typewriter that I was thrilled (and fortunate) to have—a
gift from my parents. Some weeks there were only twelve
patients in the hospital. Other weeks, there might be
twenty-seven. Some prayers filled only half the card. Others took every line of available space. But each was a sin-
cere effort at service and ministry on the part of George's
grandmother. And the more cards I typed,
the more I understood that each person's part makes a

difference in God's world. I think that is what gave me the energy to sit up late those Saturday nights and roll those cards through my typewriter.

Mrs. Teague was a beautiful woman with lovely silver hair, but it is not her physical beauty that blesses my life to this day. It is her spirit and her determination to give what she could for as long as she could, fully believing that God would honor what she gave. That's what I remember. That, and those precious, holy moments on the phone when I heard her say, "Our prayer for this week will be . . ."

Mary Stedham

8

ON GRATITUDE

Enter into his gates with thanksgiving and into his courts with praise: Be thankful unto him and bless his name.

Psalms 100:4

My Little Buddy

Most people's first jobs are pretty boring and anything but glamorous. Mine fit the stereotype exactly. But I stuck with it and plugged along day after day, year after year— for three years, six months and five days, to be exact. When asked how work was going, I had my typical responses: "I hate it," "I despise it," or my favorite, "It sucks." My first job wasn't as a waitress at the local diner or a cashier at K-Mart. No, my working days started early. When I was ten years old, I became a delivery girl for the local paper.

It wasn't so much the work I hated. Who can complain about taking one hour out of each day to throw papers on porches? No, it wasn't hard work; it was just lonely. I barely had interaction with any of my customers, and it made my job seem pointless, or unappreciated, at the very least. I delivered through pouring rain, scorching heat, snow and, even once, a hailstorm. I went through the motions day after day. I rarely got a hello from a friendly resident of the neighborhood; at times, I wondered if there even *was* a friendly resident beyond those porches. After one long June day of the same boring routine, I prayed—

hard. I prayed that the job would liven up. For if it didn't, I was sure I was going to die of boredom and loneliness.

The next day, I raced home from school to get my paper route done so I could meet my friends later. I looked on my cover sheet and noticed two new customers. *Ugghh,* I thought. *Just what I need today.* I started my route as I would have any other day, dragging my feet and hanging my head. I came to the street of one of the new customers and searched for the house. It was the big, brick house with the SOLD sign still in the front lawn. I had walked past it many times as it stood dark and empty. It was nice to see that someone was making it a home again.

On the front porch, the new owners had hung a little wooden porch swing. And on that swing sat a little boy. He was so cute! His blond hair was neatly combed to the right side, and his big blue eyes shone like they held the stars in them. At first glance, I guessed he was five. He was so adorable, and I was happy to see his smiling face looking at me. I promptly forgot that I was in a hurry to finish my paper route. As I stretched out my arm to see if he wanted the paper, he smiled and said, "Hi!" I was pleasantly surprised; in this neighborhood, even the cats didn't seem friendly.

"Well, hi," I said. He scootched his little bottom off the swing and came to take the paper. As I stood there, arms still outstretched, he confidently moved toward me. He took the paper and, as if he had known me all his life, he put his arms around me in a hug and said, "Thank you, thank you, thank you," in a sing-songy voice. Standing there stunned, I watched as he turned and trotted back into the house yelling, "Mommy, Mommy, Mommy, the paper is here!" The rest of the route I smiled, held my head up and thought about this little boy who had just put a little happiness into my day and didn't even know it.

The next day when I began my route, I had high hopes

of seeing my little buddy again. As I approached the house, I scanned the porch, hoping to see him sitting on the swing . . . to no avail. As I reached in my bag and pulled back to launch the paper, he emerged from his house with a plate of cookies in hand. He walked over to the top step of the porch and sat. He had the same radiant smile as the day before as he patted the spot next to him. Happy that he again wanted to have interaction with me, I went over to sit on the step next to him. He handed me a cookie, took one himself and we ate. No words were spoken until we had both finished our cookies.

"Thanks," I said.

"Did you like it? Those are my mommy's famous chocolate-chip cookies. And they are the *best*."

"It was delicious," I said with a smile. "So, what's your name?"

"I'm Andrew. And who are you?" he asked, with wonder in his voice.

"Bethany. I'm Bethany."

After we ate our cookie, he took the paper, hugged me and in his song-like manner said, "Thank you, thank you, thank you."

After that day, I did my paper route with happiness in my heart and a smile on my face. Sure, I still had my bad days, but whenever I reached his house, my frown became a smile. If he was going to be at his grandma's the next day or shopping with his mom, he was sure to let me know the day before so I would know where he was. Monday was our conversation day. Every Tuesday he brought me one of his mom's famous cookies. Every Wednesday we drank a juice together. On Thursday, it was a piece of gum. On Friday, he gave me five cents. Sometimes it was five pennies, and sometimes it was a nickel, but it was always five cents to say thanks for delivering each day of the week.

On every holiday, he had a present for me, whether it

was something his mom had bought for him to give or a picture he had colored himself. Without fail, he had something to present to me. My favorite gift was the one I received on Easter. It was a cross made out of Popsicle sticks that said, "Jesus loves me, this I know . . . and he loves you, too!" It wasn't an extravagant gift, but one that came from the heart and let me know I was appreciated.

Even if he wasn't going to be there, he left my treasure on the porch swing in a box. He became my "little buddy," and I became his "big buddy." Each day he was home, he would greet me with his "Hey, big buddy!" and wait for my reply of, "Hey, little buddy!" Then he would hand me my treasure, and we would exchange a few words about how his day was going or what he was up to. I would hand over his paper, and he would hug me and say, "Thank you, thank you, thank you." It never changed.

I'm sure my "little buddy" never realized what he did for me. I'm sure my "little buddy" had no idea that because of him I was able to hold my head high and smile for an hour each day, regardless of how bad the rest of the day had been. My "little buddy" taught me many things. The radiant smile that never left his face taught me how far a simple gesture can go. His presents taught me that big things really do come in small packages. And his hugs taught me that even the most insignificant jobs in life can mean something to someone.

Bethany Couts

Marking the Trail

I sat in the front pew holding hands with my mom and sister as the choir sang, "I go before you always, come follow me...." I took a few deep breaths to quiet my pounding heart and allowed my mind to wander to one of my favorite memories.

I loved that early morning hike with Dad. The smell of Rocky Mountain pine and the chilly air filled me with energy as I hustled behind him on the trail. I had hiked with Dad a dozen times in my eleven years, but I still worried when the trail disappeared.

"Is there a trail, Dad? I can't find it." I ducked under the aspen branch he held back with his large, sturdy frame. "The scouts and their dads following us are never gonna find us," I said, with mixed delight and concern. "If you weren't here, how would I ever find the way?"

He gave my shoulder a reassuring squeeze. "We'll mark our trail."

On his instruction, I gathered rocks and stacked them in a pile. Next, we arranged stones to form an arrow pointing uphill. "This shows anybody behind us which way to go," he coached.

Around the next bend I collected stones and formed them in another small heap. "Now they can follow us easily," I beamed.

We repeated these rock formations several times as I panted and stumbled over the steep terrain, following his big footprints in the soft dirt.

Feeling more exhilarated than tired, we reached the summit. There we sat in silence on the rocky peak listening to nature's concert. Wildflowers blanketed the meadow stretching between the rolling foothills. Dad gestured toward an eagle soaring in the cobalt sky.

I knew my dad created these moments especially for me. I was always the youngest scout and frequently missed out on adventures my older brother and sister experienced. Dad loved his role as an adult leader because it allowed him to combine the three loves of his life—family, faith and the great outdoors.

Storm clouds gathered over a faraway ridge. Thunder rumbled as the distant clouds collided in a clash of lightning.

"Did I ever tell you about how I *really* found God during the war?" Dad asked, breaking the silence. I knew he enjoyed telling that story almost as much I as enjoyed hearing it over and over again.

I knew it by heart. He had taken a break from maintaining the generators that provided electricity for his platoon. Sitting atop a hill, he watched the Earth burning in patches below. When a magnificent lightning storm illuminated the blackened sky, he realized no man-made electricity could compare to that of the Divine Creator. "That's when I *knew*, and I have never doubted Him since," Dad nodded with a smile.

I reached for his hand and held it tight as we watched power sparks in the distance.

When he said it was time to leave, I groaned in protest. I didn't want this treasured moment to end. He reminded me that, while we loved the trail, there are often better things at the end. "Like Mom and her pancakes waiting back at camp!"

Before beginning our trek back, Dad arranged rocks in a circle then placed a single rock in the center. "This marks the end of the trail," he said. "This will tell those who follow that we went home."

Several years later, Dad was diagnosed with Lou Gehrig's disease. His most difficult path of life lay ahead. We learned all we could about the incurable, debilitating illness, while Dad's ability to eat and speak gradually diminished. Accepting his impending death with courage and faith, he still showed me the way.

He led me through earning my Eagle Scout award.

I followed in his footsteps when I was confirmed in my faith.

He guided me through the rocky path of high-school graduation and choosing a college.

He gathered me with my mom, grandma, aunt and uncle to pray together after church every Sunday.

In written notes, he told us that, while he loved life's journey, he looked forward to eternity with the Master Electrician.

My sister tugged gently on my hand. The choir ended the refrain, and the piano played softly as Father Bob offered the final funeral prayer. Dozens of scouts and former scouts came forward, placing a circle of rocks on the altar. Together my sister, brother and I placed the single rock in the center.

It was the end of the trail.

Dad had gone home.

Tim Chaney
As told to LeAnn Thieman

Pulse

I am not an unusual teenager. I've never been given an award for anything special or nominated for an important position. I've had my share of problems and, like most teenage girls, spent countless nights crying over lost friendships, unrequited love and just everyday teenage stress.

One night I was watching a show on TV about an angel. The angel was trying to convince one of the characters not to kill himself. The man thought that dying was the easiest way out. I thought about how many times I have considered the same thing. I put my finger up to my pulse. A thought struck me: This is what will keep me alive. No matter how many breakups I go through, no matter how many times my "dream" soccer team rejects me and no matter how many times I can't pull off my I'm-tough-and-I-don't-cry attitude, that pulse will still be there. Blood will still be pumped through my body. I can survive.

This isn't to say that I will never think about quitting or never go through a day where all hope seems to be lost. But there is one thing I know for sure: In the times of greatest sorrow, or melancholy, or hopelessness, or lifelessness, I only need to use one finger to know that I can survive it all. The steady flow of my healthy, thirteen-year-old heart is the most comforting feeling in the world.

Adrianna Hutchinson

THE FAMILY CIRCUS®   By Bil Keane

©BKi

"Can't wait till I'm a teenager and I can do anything I want and not have anything to worry about."

Reprinted with permission of Bil Keane.

Good-Bye, Pollywogs

Just a shimmering shadow of femininity at age twelve, I'd dart toward young womanhood to enjoy—for a fleeting moment—the taste and feel of lipstick and heels. Tentatively, I'd flirt with a boy, then rush back to my childish, tomboy self and hang by my legs from a tree, make funny faces or wallow in the pond-side mud to catch a pollywog. The transition to teenager was tough, but sickness, a sweater and first love made it happen.

The Connecticut Police Athletic League (PAL), with its offerings of field trips to New York City, Yale football games, picnics and Sunday evening block parties on the village green, gave me and most other kids in my hometown opportunities to blow off steam. Boredom was rare; the PAL had activities every day for all seasons.

Sergeant Mahoney loved me. And I loved him—his round Irish face, booming voice and, most of all, his sixteen-year-old son. While Sarge was the founder, fundraiser and CEO of our PAL chapter, his son, Mickey, with his wide, freely given smile and all-American good looks, kept us all energized with baseball and football. Gawky and goofy, I rarely got his attention, unless I hit a home run or won the tournament relay race.

Mickey always wore his PAL sweater, and I noticed the other kids were wearing them, too. I wanted one. I saw a sense of belonging, an imagined kinship with the high-school girls who looked so cool in their sweaters. I watched those bigger girls closely, every nuance of behavior, the shape of their plucked eyebrows and hairstyles, and their smooth-shaven legs.

I talked to my mom about these things and the sweater, woman to woman. Mom knew a girl who wore makeup over her acne; she got an infection and died. Mom had a friend who shaved her legs, got an infection and died. Another of Mom's friends ran in the heat; she got polio and died. Instead of advice and money, Mom gave me an obituary. But I was already infected—with sweater desire. If clothes make the man, the PAL sweater would make me a member of some elusive teenage thing. I longed to belong.

The cost of the sweater was high. I got on my bike and collected recyclables, did extra chores and even raked our neighbor's horse barn. Odiferous, but richer, I gained permission to take the bus after school and make this important purchase.

I woke up on the appointed morning and felt kind of weird. I figured it was just anticipation and left for school. As the day eased toward noon, my anticipation degenerated into fever. I was sick. But I couldn't let illness thwart my plan; this was the day, and my sweater waited. Somehow, I staggered home for lunch and managed to pretend wellness. I was good at this. Earlier that year, I'd made it to a PAL dance with the measles. With no rash to hide, this was going to be easy, I thought. I walked the two blocks back to school in a feverish daze. It was the longest day of my young life as I begged my friends not to tell our teacher I was sick.

Finally, I boarded the bus and dozed until we arrived in the city. Refreshed and eager, I barely noticed my churning stomach as I hurried past many storefronts until I found the "official" sport shop. There they were, beige stacks of neatly folded, thickly knit club sweaters. I tried on three sizes. To achieve a really cool effect, the sweater must hang toward the back of my knees and the cuff should be folded at least twice. Extra large was perfect. And now for the PAL logo and my name. Reverently, I caressed the green, velvety letters as the man rang up my sale. "Do you want this in a box?" he asked. "Oh, I'll wear it now, thank you." I stuffed my old jacket in a bag and left.

You know how after a long-distance race the runners collapse at the finish line? After a channel swim the swimmer reaches land and falls, exhausted, on the shore. That was me, on the sidewalk outside the shop—exhilarated, exhausted and sick as can be. The challenge to get home wasn't exactly a driving force. I felt queasy and feverish, and I wanted my mom. My stomach rumbled and my legs shook as weakness consumed me. I'd walk a bit, hang onto a light post and rest. Time was running out; the last bus home left at five o'clock. I tried to hurry. Finally, my stomach gave a mighty roar, and I threw up in the street, leaning far over so I wouldn't stain my wonderful new sweater.

Slowly, I forged across the desert of downtown. People began to notice as I staggered along, yet no one helped. I arrived at the bus stop just as the bus pulled away from the curb. With the last drop of adrenaline in my body, I shouted and ran, and the bus stopped. There is a God.

I wearily climbed aboard the crowded bus and hung onto the overhead strap. Only the strength of my clinging arms kept me upright; my legs were long, thin strands of Jell-O. The bus swayed, bumped and rocked. I prayed, wished and clenched my teeth, but the dreaded moment arrived. I lunged for the tiny stairwell and was sick again. Like a cowering dog, I feared to look at the poor passengers subjected to my selfish sweater desires. Then I felt gentle arms pull and push me carefully to the back of the bus. Someone got up, and I was laid on the seat. A big, heavyset woman with a bandana on her head put an arm around me and eased my head onto her warm, lilac-scented lap. A man dipped his handkerchief into the melted ice in his thermos and placed it on my forehead. I closed my eyes and listened to concerned murmurs of angels and the restful humming of the big lady's voice. The bus driver knew me and my stop. He drove right up to my driveway, and a strong young man carried me to my porch and to my mom.

Just before he released me, Sergeant Mahoney's son, Mickey, whispered in my ear, "You look really cute in that sweater." I opened my eyes and, for the first time in my life, I smiled demurely and spoke in a new, feminine voice, "Why, thank you."

My tomboy days were over, and I never chased pollywogs again.

Lynne Zielinski

"The Bell Choir would like you to continue serving
as their director . . . but only if you promise
to stop calling them your 'little dingalings'."

The Gift of Life

For you created my inmost being; you knit me together in my mother's womb. I praise you because I am fearfully and wonderfully made; your works are wonderful, I know that full well.

Psalms 139:13–14

It is that time of year again . . . the time for rainy spring days, the smell of budding flowers and the sound of chatter on the softball field.

As I watch the tear-stained eighteen-year-old, I want to hug out all of the sadness and frustration she is feeling and tell her how much I love her. Tonight may be the last softball game of her high-school career—a career cut short because a nagging knee injury needs surgery so that she can be ready to fulfill her athletic scholarship at college. As I gaze upon her face, I cannot help but think of how fortunate I have been to know this beautiful young lady. However, I know how easily her song could have been one that was unsung. . . .

It was almost nineteen years ago that a teenager

trembled as she tearfully said to her mother and father the words that every parent dreads: "Mom, Dad, I'm pregnant."

What a frightening time for a nineteen-year-old as she is just starting her adult life and already facing an uncertain future. What devastation for the parents as this is the last thing they would have chosen for their daughter. Thoughts of, *We have failed her* to *I am too young to be grandparents*, fill their minds. In a heartbeat the atmosphere in the house becomes strained, and the following nights are long for the teen as she drenches her pillow with tears—tears that come only when she thinks no one can see or hear her.

Many try to persuade her to keep her options open, but there is only one choice for this determined teen. The little life within her has now become her responsibility, and she will sacrifice all she has to see that this precious being grows to be the young man or woman God intended him or her to be. She is at peace with herself and the choice she has made.

A baby's first cries fill the air, and an exhausted but proud teenage mom holds her young daughter for the first time. She is inexperienced, but determined to provide for her priceless daughter the best way that she can. If the first few days are any indication, she has a tough hill to climb. Because she has no insurance, she leaves the hospital early and takes her daughter home, but the baby girl develops jaundice, and they are forced back to the hospital. Her pediatrician tells her to leave the baby in their care and to go home and rest. "You have got to be kidding me!" she exclaims, refusing to leave her baby girl for even a moment. Something inside her clicks and, with a determination that surpasses anything she has felt up to this point, she comes to grips with the situation. *You are a mom now. Deal with it,* she quietly tells herself.

Life is not easy, and many hopes and plans for the

future are set aside. The early years are filled with tests and trials, but it is a time in her life that she wouldn't trade for anything. During those rough days and nights, she need only look at this tender creation God has given her to realize that the best things in life are right before her in the smile, the coo and the laugh of this darling baby girl.

Those eighteen years have flown by, and I ponder all of these things as we slowly walk away from the softball diamond today. I think about all the joy this baby girl, who is now a young woman herself, has brought into my life and to those around her. I remember all the basketball and softball games that we as her family have sat through, proudly cheering her on. Not only is she the best all-around female athlete I have ever seen, but she is also one of the classiest, and I am most proud of who she is off the court. She conducts herself with grace and humility and shows kindness to all who cross her path. I cannot imagine life without my Jen, my darling eighteen-year-old niece.

Tonight my heart is bursting with pride, love and joy for this remarkable being who came into our lives. I shudder to think if she had not been born. How different our family would have been, not to mention the lives of an untold number of people whom she has touched in her everyday life.

A scared but determined teenage mom made a tough decision all those years ago, and through it, gave us all the gift of Jen.

Kristi Powers

Daddy's Hug

"On numerous occasions my eyes have beheld the incredible beauty which you do so glamorously possess. We must meet and we will in the very near future."

I vividly remember the handwriting on the card, although I can't quite recall what the flowers looked like. They may have been roses or perhaps carnations. No matter. They were the first flowers I had ever received from a secret admirer. Actually, they were the first flowers I had received from anyone besides my dad.

In high school, I was a bit awkward. I felt like the lone Olive Oyl in a sea full of Betty Boops. I was the girl who counseled all the boys on what kind of flowers to buy the other girls, but I never received any of my own. I was friend material, not girlfriend material.

But then I went away to college. No one there knew I used to be tall and lanky and covered with corrective appliances because now I had contacts. My retainer was long gone, and there was a good chance I was moving into the girlfriend zone. The fact that I had just received flowers from a secret admirer was very encouraging.

Using clever detective skills, I compared the hand-writing on the card to the roll sheets in my classes and discovered my secret admirer was in my radio-production class. As luck would have it, I thought he was quite cute, and my eyes had been "beholding" him, too. I got brave and approached him after class one day, trying to surprise him with my cleverness.

"Thank you for the flowers," I said, nonchalantly.

"How did you know it was me?" he asked. He sounded disappointed. Not a good sign. "I was planning on over-whelming you with more, but since you know it was me. . . ."

"I'm sorry," I interrupted. "I must have mistaken you for someone else." I tried to back away.

Too late. I had discovered him and ruined his plan. There was nothing to do now but go out on an actual date. So off we went to play miniature golf, and although I can't remember who won, I remember we had a great time.

I remember thinking what a great story we would have to tell our grandchildren. But all romances have an element of tragedy, and our story turned tragic the very next day. As I was floating on air to my afternoon class, I crashed to the ground when I saw my secret admirer kissing another girl in front of my dorm.

To be honest, my heart was in a fragile state. Too many lonely Friday nights had weakened it already. Now it was completely broken. Not just over this guy, but over all the boys who had failed to see me as the girl I wanted them to see.

I did the only thing I knew to do: I went home to Mom. But it was not my mom who met me at the door. It was my dad. I don't remember him saying a word. He simply held me and let me cry. Even as I mourned my singleness, I treasured the comfort of Daddy's arms. Soon all the tears were dry, but Daddy still held me.

I honestly can't remember when my dad and I had

shared a moment like that before, and I have nothing but gratitude for the guy who broke my heart so that my dad could pick up the pieces.

Since that day, my secret admirer and I have become "just friends." My heart was broken a couple more times before I gave it to the man who became my husband. As for my dad, he did much more than just comfort me that day. He taught me a great lesson. When life gets tough, which it has a time or two, all I need to do is turn to God, the real Father. The peace and love I find in His arms somehow makes me thankful for the trials that sent me there.

Melanie Walenciak

$\overline{9}$

ON BLESSINGS AND MIRACLES

And all these blessings shall come on thee and overtake thee if thou shalt hearken unto the voice of the Lord thy God.

Deuteronomy 28:2

Walking by Faith

I can do all things through Christ who strengthens me.

Philippians 4:13

I'll never forget the day I met her and her glowing personality. It was the beginning of my senior year of high school. I had that typical senior attitude—I was anxious, excited, a little on the proud side. I wanted to enjoy my senior year, and I wasn't too concerned with meeting or befriending any lowerclassmen, especially not the new kids. Fortunately, my arrogance was overcome the moment I met Sarah in my computer class on the first day of school. There was just something about her. She was so friendly and sweet, and seemed genuinely excited about being at our tiny eighty-student Christian high school.

It was only ten minutes of initial small talk that endeared Sarah to my heart. She liked basketball. Basketball was one of the highlights of my childhood, and our slightly weak team was always thrilled to welcome new players.

She was taller than me by a couple of inches, and my

five-foot-seven frame was unfortunately the tallest on our team. Each practice, as we worked together toward our common goal, we became closer. She was always so encouraging and positive; it seemed like nothing could get her down.

I remember vividly an early tournament we attended that December. We were playing a team that was tough. They had been our rivals throughout my basketball years. The game went back and forth, and victory was up for grabs. However, it looked like our team would not pull through. Three of our starters had fouled out, and we were falling behind until Sarah entered the game with great enthusiasm. She played well, but it was her attitude that helped us the most. "We're going to win this!" I remember her saying. And we did! After that game, I remember admiring Sarah's determination to succeed and her powerful encouragement. She seemed to be fearless of any obstacle she might have to face.

Unfortunately, in only a matter of weeks, she would have to face a life-changing one. Sarah was involved in a terrible car accident on her way to school. During a bad snowstorm, her family's van skidded off the road, and Sarah was thrown several feet onto the pavement. Her major injuries included a crushed vertebrae in her neck and a bruised spine. For a day or two, no one knew if she would survive. Then the doctors told her that she would never walk again.

As soon as I heard the tragic news, my heart sank. Why did this happen to someone like Sarah? My spirits were instantly lifted, however, as I watched classmates, friends and teachers earnestly praying for Sarah's recovery. It wasn't until a few weeks later when a couple of my friends and I visited Sarah in the hospital that I realized the extent of her positive attitude. She had impacted her family, friends, our basketball team and even the nurses with her faith in God and her strong will to recover completely. Despite the doctor's negative prognosis, Sarah remained calm and determined. Her faith never wavered, even though those of us who loved her most doubted that walking would ever be in her future. Sarah put herself 100 percent into getting better and walking on her own. When she wasn't doing painful rehabilitation exercises, she was either spreading her kindness to others or praying.

It wasn't long before Sarah was indeed walking again. She showed the same strength and devotion toward getting better as she did each time she walked onto the basketball court. She isn't playing basketball yet, but I don't doubt that she will be amazing us once again. Sometimes just believing can make anything possible.

Corinne Ingram

[AUTHOR'S NOTE: *Sarah now attends a Christian college in southern Florida. The last time I saw her was at a varsity basketball game at our former high school. Of all the people who I wanted to see during my Christmas break, she was at the top of my list. We greeted each other with a big hug, and she had that same big smile on her face—that smile that even after all she had been through, still shone courageously. She had completed her first semester of her freshman year and would be returning after break to continue her education in writing.*]

Daddy's Miracle

*F*aith the size of a mustard seed can move a mountain.

Matthew 17:20

Two days after my fifteenth birthday, my life changed forever. My mother woke me at five that morning to prepare me for the sirens and ambulances on the way. My father had had a stroke. That's when the nightmare began, and it continued to haunt me for weeks. All I could do was pray.

My sixth-grade teacher once said, "God draws straight with crooked lines." I didn't think of it then much, but I understood later how God turns the worst experiences into miraculous events.

The doctors didn't expect my father to survive that day, but God had a different plan. When news of the stroke got out, support came from everywhere. It was the beginning of the straight line yet to be drawn.

While my dad was in a coma for about a month, I saw family, friends, neighbors and people I have never even met come together in prayer. It was most difficult at school. People really couldn't understand what I was going through. My teacher was amazed at my progress despite the conditions at home, but my dad had taught me to never be satisfied, that there is always room for improvement. I told her he wouldn't want me to fall apart, and I had no intention of doing so.

As time went on, Dad slowly came out of his coma, but it was months before he came home. Several holidays were spent in hospitals, and I began to grow aggravated with those who complained about their families. At least their parents were healthy. One day I saw a sign on Dad's hospital bed that said, "Okay to return to service." Many would think it applied to the bed, but I knew it was God's way of telling me everything would be okay. Dad's work was not yet complete.

There were still nights I would lie in bed just praying that God would make it all go away and restore my life to how it was. I still had faith, but I never thought that my request would be heard. He proved me wrong.

It was time for my youth retreat. My mom and dad were always very active in youth ministries, but I debated about going on this retreat. It wouldn't be the same without them, but something inside me urged me to go. So I did. A fellow peer leader asked if she could do a talk on my father. I didn't see why not. When it came time for the talk, she went on by saying how this man had had such an impact on her life. By the end I was in tears, but it wasn't long before fifteen new-found friends were by my side surrounding me with hugs. That's when I knew my dad had given me a piece of heaven. After Sunday mass the church donated money to my family, and my dad was there to see his teachings in action.

A friend of the family then did a fund-raiser to help pay for the addition that had to be built on our home. It was amazing how many people cared. Thanks to them, my dad is now back home.

All the nights I had prayed for just one more hug or one more smile paid off. Although he can't do all the things he used to, Dad still manages to bring smiles to everyone's face. It's amazing how far a little faith can go. I now take more time to see what's important in life. I don't let life's adversities bring me down; instead, I try to face them with a smile and make each day the best day of my life. God truly does draw straight with crooked lines.

Jenny DeYaeger

"Dad, I don't have sex, I don't use drugs,
I don't swear, and I don't drink alcohol.
But still, I *am* a teenager and I have a
natural desire to be a little rebellious.
Is it okay if I call you 'Baldy' once in a while?"

Reprinted by permission of Randy Glasbergen.

Death Wave

It was five-thirty in the morning, and I was fast asleep.
Plink. Plink.
I was dreaming about waves, perfect rides.
Plink. Plink. Plink.
I was drifting between my glorious dreams and consciousness.
Plink. Plunk!
Startled, my eyes popped open.

It must be Matt, I thought. Moving quickly, I opened my second-story window, knowing Matt was outside. "I'll be down in a minute," I whispered loudly.

This was all part of our pre-dawn ritual; as surfing buddies, we had a system. Whoever woke up first had to wake the other. My room was upstairs, so Matt had to throw pebbles at my window to wake me.

Bicycling toward the beach, we left our sleeping neighborhood behind. Rounding the corner to the beach entrance, we could hear the gentle crashing sound of the waves. As we got closer, the sounds grew louder. In the dead of the morning, the waves seemed to call us with their rhythmic voices, one after another, *"Kishhh, kishhh . . . kishhh."*

Walking across the beach toward the water, our senses were filled with the smell of saltwater and the increasing sound of breaking waves. We entered the water up to our waists, and with our boards by our sides we stood watching and calculating. We silently stared as if frozen in the predawn darkness.

Finally, I yelled "Now!" and we jumped on our boards and began paddling out to sea. For waves this size, timing was critical. Sets of waves would come in, one after another. But every so often there would be a slight lull in the sets. This was our chance. If we paddled hard and fast, we could make it out to the break line and not get caught by the surf that would push us back to shore.

As rays from the rising sun began peeking over the mountains, Matt and I made it out to the break line. It was an awesome day. The waves were large, about eight to ten feet high.

The first wave came in quickly. To my disappointment, Matt had better positioning and caught the wave, riding it to shore. I watched him for a while before turning back toward the sea. Soon enough there was another wave forming and coming right at me. *Awesome,* I thought, *this one is mine.* I started paddling to meet it. As I paddled, I noticed it was larger than the rest. I started paddling a little harder. *Oh, man, this one's big,* I thought. As I got closer to the oncoming wave, I realized it was enormous. On a day with surf around eight to ten feet high, this wave seemed twice that size. *Paddle, paddle!* I thought to myself. *I've got to get over this wave!*

As I feverishly paddled with all of my strength, the wave began to crest in front of me. Sucking me toward it as it swelled, I knew I wasn't going to make it over. Normally, the best thing to do would be to ditch my board and try to swim for the ocean bottom. This would keep the wave from breaking directly on my head, thus insulating me from the brunt of the wave's power. However, this would not keep me from the unavoidable turbulence that would drag me underwater for long seconds, or in the case of this large wave, probably minutes. But it was my only choice.

As time stood still, I let go of my surfboard. I took a deep breath, figuring I would be under for a long time. Then I glanced up to see the cresting lip of the enormous wave rushing toward me. Engulfed with fear, I thought it was the end. My mind and heart yelled, *Oh, God, help!* Then I dove.

Meanwhile, Matt was watching this whole episode unfold from the shore. Knowing I was in danger, he turned his board toward the sea and with each stroke of his arms prayed, *Oh, God, let him be all right. Oh, God, please let him be all right.*

As Matt fought the surf, he finally made it out to the break line. A little further out he saw my surfboard. Matt turned his board and paddled toward it. As he got closer, he could see the top of my head next to my board. *Oh, God, let him be alive. Please let him still be alive.*

Getting closer, Matt couldn't believe his eyes. I was treading water with my arm draped over my board. I seemed to be all right. "Are you okay? Are you all right?" Matt shouted.

Dazed, I slowly turned my head toward my friend. Then after a moment, I said softly, "Yeah, I'm fine. I'm fine."

"What happened?" Matt demanded. "You were an ant compared to that wave. I thought you were done. I thought it was going to kill you."

"I don't know," I said with quiet amazement. "I thought I was dead, too. But the wave . . . it didn't hurt me, it didn't even take me . . . it just disappeared, I think."

"Well, it broke right on top of you. I saw it. Were you under for a long time?" Matt asked.

"No. One minute the wave was breaking, and the next I was treading water with my surfboard right next to me," I answered, with astonishment in my voice.

"That's impossible!" Matt said, shaking his head.

"I know," I replied quietly, "I know."

Michael Ambrosio

Charmed Life

Don't believe in miracles—depend on them.

Laurence J. Peter

I've often been told I lead a charmed life. Most of the time, the people who tell me this are my parents because they want me to be especially appreciative of something they have done for me. I was really appreciative when, before my sixteenth birthday, my dad took me out to pick out a car for a present! I had always dreamed of having my own car, and I really couldn't believe it was happening even when my dad and I went to the car dealership, and I chose a Mitsubishi Mirage Coupe. It was white with a leather interior. I thought it was the coolest car around. Even when my friend John got a black Nissan Maxima for his birthday, I thought mine was the best.

The night of my birthday, we went out to dinner—the whole family. My grandparents gave me a watch, a real beauty with all kinds of functions like a telephone book and games. I was certainly not expecting anything else since my parents had given me a car! So I was very

surprised when my mother handed me a small box. Inside
was a long silver chain with a St. Christopher's medal on
it. It had belonged to my mother's father who died before
I was born. My mother said the medal always protected
him. He was a soldier in World War II, and he wore that
medal all the time. I guess St. Christopher couldn't save
him from a heart attack, though, a few years after my parents were married. I thanked everyone, put on my new
watch and slipped the medal around my neck. Of course,
I tucked it inside my shirt.

My friend John and I took turns driving to school. Monday he would drive; Tuesday I would drive. We also took
turns driving to work. Since we both had to pay for car
insurance, we got part-time jobs at the grocery store.

John was a faster driver than I was. It's not that he ever
sped. He knew his father would take away the car if he got
a ticket. But he just had a heavier foot than I did. My dad
told me that it was hard on the brake linings to hit them
hard. I wanted my car to last forever. It was my "baby" so
I treated it gently.

On one of John's mornings to drive, I was just getting out
of the shower when I heard him honk. That was when I
remembered him telling me that he had to get to school
early to make up a biology test. I asked my mother to call out
to him that I was running late, and I would drive myself. She
told me John said he would wait. He stayed in the car, listening to his music. When I looked out the window, I could
see him drumming, as he always did, on his steering wheel.

I had my coat on and was out the door when I realized I
had forgotten my calculator. I motioned to John that I had
to go back up for a minute, and I dashed up the stairs. I
thought I had left my calculator on my dresser, but the only
thing there was my St. Christopher's medal. I don't know
why I did it because I didn't wear it all the time, but I picked
up the necklace and slipped it on. Then I remembered: My

calculator was in my coat pocket! I patted my coat just to make sure, and there it was. I ran back down the stairs, grabbed my books and opened the front door.

But John wasn't there. I thought he probably didn't understand my hand signal and assumed I would drive myself.

About a mile from school, I heard the first siren. It sounded far off so I didn't pull over. The next sirens, though, came from behind me. I looked in my rearview mirror and saw fire engines and a police car. I joined the other cars pulled over on the right side of the road.

I guess seeing all those emergency vehicles scream past made me a little jumpy, but I couldn't help thinking of John and how he didn't want to be late that morning. I opened my car door and stood up to see if I could see the accident that was causing the holdup. All I saw were three police cars forming a blockade at the top of the hill. Traffic was being rerouted. I would be late for school, but I was sure that a lot of other kids and probably some teachers would be, too.

Traffic inched up the hill. As I got closer, I looked over to see the accident. I knew it was rubbernecking, but I couldn't help it. I wished I hadn't. Across the road, jack-knifed, was a huge moving van. It was in an odd place, just below the crest of the hill. Smashed up against it were two cars. Both of them were black. I couldn't tell what make and model they were, but I didn't need to. Somehow I knew that one of those cars belonged to John. The police report, when we read it later, said that the truck had jackknifed, making a left turn just below the hill. The drivers of the two cars racing each other over the crest couldn't see the van stalled across the street until they had topped the rise. By then, it was too late to stop.

Shaking, I pulled over to the side of the road, all thoughts of getting to school on time forgotten. I called my dad on my cell phone. I was so upset, I could barely get the words out. My dad thought I had had the accident! When he finally understood that John and I were in separate cars and that John had had the accident, he told me to go to the emergency room behind the ambulances. He would meet me there.

I had a hard time getting the key in the ignition, turning it and shifting into gear. My hands shook. I was afraid of what I would see at the hospital. Most of all, I didn't want to do this alone. As I reached over to shift the gear, something clinked against the steering wheel. I looked down to see my St. Christopher's medal dangling out of my shirt. I think that was the moment I said a prayer. Clutching the medal in my left hand, I worked the shift and prayed that my best friend and I would laugh about this later. I imagined how angry his dad would be and how I would have to drive John everywhere. His dad would make him pay for the car. I prayed hard that this would be the outcome—just an angry father and an unhurt friend.

I reached the hospital just before John's parents. His mom saw me and ran to hug me. She thought I had been in the car with him. And if I was okay, she hoped her son was, too. I hated to tell her that I had driven my own car that morning. I told her I had seen the accident after it happened. I didn't tell her what John's car had looked like.

They weren't sure which of the two drivers was John. One of them was very badly hurt; he hadn't been wearing a seat belt. The nurse took John's mother into the inner area while I waited outside. Suddenly, my knees turned to jelly. I was alone in the waiting room, and I was afraid. Once more, I reached for the medal and said a hasty prayer.

The big double doors opened, and John's father stepped out. "He's going to be okay!" John's dad said. He hugged me tight. "Thank God you boys know to wear your seat belts!"

They wouldn't let me see him, and I knew I should go to school even if I was going to be late. But I couldn't. I drove home.

That's when it hit me. John hated wearing a seat belt! He almost never wore one! But he must have been wearing one or . . . I didn't want to think about it. I couldn't get the picture of the smashed black car out of my mind.

My mother came home from work early. By three o'clock, the news of the accident was all over town. My mother hugged me. (That made twice in one day I had let a grown-up do that!) She looked at me carefully.

"When I think that it could have been you in that car with him . . . Oh, Daniel, I'm so glad you decided to drive yourself this morning." For the second time that day I felt my knees go weak, and I sat down on the couch.

"I was late. And then I forgot my calculator. I ran back to get it. I thought I had left it on my dresser, but it was in my coat pocket. The only thing on my dresser was . . ." I felt a sudden chill even as I said the words, slowly ". . . my St. Christopher's medal." My mother looked at me with perfect understanding. But then another thought occurred to me. I said, "When I came down, John had gone. Mom, I made him wait for me a little while. I made him late! That was why he was driving so fast! It was my fault!"

Sixteen years old, and I couldn't help crying.

But then my mother said, "John was racing the driver of the other car, Daniel. He made the choice to do that. You had nothing to do with it. John's mother told me that it was a miracle that John had his seat belt on. That was what saved him. That, his air bag and the grace of God."

I think we both knew who had saved me. If I hadn't gone back up to my room, if I had felt that calculator in the pocket of my coat before I reached my room . . . I never would have picked up the necklace and put it on. I would have gotten outside in time to ride with John.

My mother was half-right. John was saved by the belt, the air bag, God and St. Christopher!

I was allowed to see John two days later. He was bruised from the air bag. His hands, arms, face and chest were black and blue. But nothing was broken. I had to ask, "What made you put that seat belt on, John?"

He looked at me strangely. "I don't know, Daniel," he said. "It was just a feeling I had when I left your house. You know I never put it on, man. I hate having it across me; it's uncomfortable. But for some reason—and I didn't even think about it then—when I pulled out of your driveway, I just put it on. Well, I'm gonna think about it now. I might be dumb, but I'm not stupid!"

I don't know why I did it, and I don't know why John didn't tell me not to. He hates jewelry, but I slipped my necklace off and put it around John's neck. He didn't even ask me what I was doing. He just thanked me. I think both of us knew.

My mother was right; I do lead a charmed life. But I wanted my best friend to lead one, too. I bought myself another medal with the money I made working at the grocery store.

Cool or not, we both wear our seat belts now when we drive. We never know when St. Chris might decide to take the bus.

Name Withheld
As told to Marsha Arons

E-MAIL:CLOSETOHOME@COMPUSERVE.COM 6-1

www.uexpress.com

© 1998 John McPherson/Dist. by Universal Press Syndicate

"Adding you to our car insurance as a teenager will triple our rate. From now on, wear this mask and overcoat, and go by the name 'Uncle Mort.'"

A Divine Purpose

It appears I am destined for something; I will live.

Robert Clive

"My back hurts. Do you see a bruise or something?" I asked my mom on the way home from a track meet on a Friday afternoon. It had been a pretty good day, but I hadn't felt well from the start. There was a flu going around school, so I figured I was coming down with it. But I just couldn't understand this horrible pulling pain in my back. We decided it was probably just a pulled muscle from the track meet.

On Sunday, my temperature spiked to 104.5 degrees. We didn't go to church. Instead, we were trying to figure out what to do next when my mom got up from the couch, got her medical reference book and began to read. She asked me some questions, and I answered yes to all of them. The questions were all about appendicitis. She called a nurse, who advised we go to the doctor's office the following morning.

I didn't sleep well that night due to the pain. The next day we went to the doctor's office, they ran some tests and determined that my appendix had ruptured. Although she believed that it had ruptured on Friday night, she explained that my body had secured a pouch in which the poison had pocketed itself off instead of traveling through my body. We went straight to the children's hospital. Once there, I was examined by lots of doctors who determined that I needed immediate surgery. Afterwards, the surgeon told my parents they had removed it just in time.

In the days following my operation, my surgeon came to check on me. We developed a friendship after I told her I also wanted to be a surgeon who helped children. She told me she would help by inviting me to come and watch surgeries. I have gone many times since. During these visits, I have had the chance to talk to medical students and residents. I have been able to formulate a plan for volunteer work and for college. Most importantly, though, the experiences I've had have strengthened my desire to follow my dream. It is an awesome thing to know that healing can come through the hands of a surgeon. Even more awesome for me is knowing that someday I will be the one standing at that operating table giving children the help they need. As the saying goes, God works in mysterious ways. I know that my life was saved for a divine purpose.

Nathan Roy

Blessed

I will praise the name of God with a song and will magnify him with thanksgiving.

Psalms 69:30

Whitney stepped up to the microphone to sing the National Anthem. Her voice was strong and clear, and the high-school gym erupted into cheers as she sang the last notes and the basketball teams dashed onto the court. But the loudest cheers in the stadium came from her greatest fans—her father, Tony, her older brother, Jared, and me, her grateful mother.

I never dreamed we'd be sitting here again, I thought, my heart bursting with pride as my daughter took her place with the other high-school cheerleaders. *After everything she's been through, it's a miracle Whitney is still alive.*

Our long nightmare began when Whitney came down with what seemed like a simple sinus infection. After complaining of a sore throat, her doctor prescribed antibiotics, but they didn't help at all.

Whitney's glands swelled. Her whole body grew stiff

and achy. I guessed she might be coming down with the flu and put her to bed. But over the next several days, Whitney's condition took an unexpected turn for the worse. Her hands and feet began to tingle . . . and soon the tip of her nose was tingling, too.

One night, Whitney noticed her upper lip was going numb. The next morning when she awoke, her eyes were crossed and she was seeing double.

We rushed Whitney to our family doctor, who immediately sent her to a neurologist. At the hospital, doctors put Whitney in quarantine and performed a spinal tap. Whitney frantically asked what was wrong with her as she continued to lose feeling in her limbs and face.

She was finally diagnosed with meningoencephalitis and Guillain-Barré syndrome. The doctor told us it is very rare to have either condition; to have both is almost unheard of.

The delicate membrane that was supposed to cushion Whitney's brain was swollen and causing painful pressure. Her motor nerves had been stripped of their protective lining, and her arms and legs were growing weaker by the minute. She couldn't walk or feed herself, or move the muscles in her face to make any expression at all.

Her doctor theorized she may have contracted the mono virus, causing her immune system to overreact and begin attacking her own body. His next words drove a spike of fear through my heart. "I'm afraid it's going to get a lot worse before it gets better."

Whitney was an honor-roll student who had made the cheerleading squad every year since she was twelve. She loved performing with her high school's choir, but as she lay in the hospital bed she wondered if she would ever sing or dance again.

Soon Whitney was transferred to the intensive-care unit, where a ventilator stood ready to help her breathe.

Her doctor explained that sometimes with Guillain-Barré, the paralysis grows so bad that even drawing a breath becomes too difficult. We needed to be prepared—just in case.

For the next three days, I sat at Whitney's bedside praying for a miracle. Whitney could barely speak, her tongue felt so numb and thick in her mouth, and her eyes were mere slits because she didn't have enough motor control to open her eyelids. Whitney's entire body was a single raw nerve, and she sobbed in agony when the pain grew so excruciating that even morphine didn't help.

Whitney's name was added to numerous prayer chains and, miraculously, she survived her respiratory crisis. We all celebrated when it was decided she wouldn't need the ventilator, and Whitney was moved out of the ICU.

Doctors prescribed physical therapy to help her regain use of her arms and legs. Whitney struggled as she tried to grip a toothbrush. When she practiced with her walker, her legs dangled limply as the physical therapist encouraged her to push against the floor.

Whitney pushed herself as hard as she could because she knew it was the only way she'd ever get well. "Look, Mom—I'm smiling," she said one day. I felt my heart break in two as I forced myself to smile back even though Whitney's face remained a frozen mask of paralyzed muscle.

But I felt a sense of hope for the first time. *Despite everything she's been through*, I thought, *Whitney's still trying to smile. She still has hope, and she's trying to pass that hope along to me.* Somehow, I knew Whitney would fight her way back from this terrible illness . . . and her strength was inspiring the rest of us to be strong.

Doctors told Whitney she'd need a wheelchair to return to school, but Whitney was determined to prove them wrong. "C'mon, Mom, let's go again," she would beg only minutes after her physical-therapy session because she wanted even more exercise with her walker.

"Go for it!" Jared said, giving his sister her handgrips and counting off the reps. "One more," he coaxed again and again. "You can do it. I know you can."

After two weeks, Whitney was transferred to St. Vincent's Children's Hospital, where she continued her therapy and received tutoring from a hospital teacher. Whitney dictated her lessons to me, but one day her hands were finally nimble enough to sign her own name to her homework paper. She beamed with pride, and this time her smile was the real thing.

We threw a big party the day Whitney came home from the hospital. After ten weeks of outpatient therapy, she returned to school—not in a wheelchair or even using a walker, but on her own two feet with only leg braces for support.

Before long, Whitney was singing again with the school choir, and by the following fall when cheerleading tryouts came around, she made the varsity squad. This year she's a member of the All-Star Team.

Whitney uses only a single word to describe how she feels today: "Blessed." Blessed for the doctors who fought to save her life. Blessed for the prayers of friends and schoolmates . . . and blessed for the family who was always there for her.

Jerrilyn Thetford
As told to Heather Black

Roses for Tara

Within your heart, keep one still, secret spot where dreams may go.

Louise Driscoll

It was a simple, two-page application, but I knew it could change my life forever. Name: Tara Steele. Birth Date: October 1, 1978. Place of Birth: North Vancouver, B.C.

Ever since I could remember, I'd always known I was adopted. But now that I was an adult, Canadian law said I could register to have my records opened and maybe find my birth mom.

Does she look like me? Would she even want to meet me? I wondered, as I sat on my bed proofreading every line. Then I folded the form and tucked it away in my purse . . . and for the next five months I carried it around, wondering if I'd ever have the nerve to mail it.

We were only seventeen and still in high school. My boyfriend, Fred, and I were too young to raise a child. We could never give a baby the life she deserved, but I still cried the day my mom and I went to the adoption agency and a caseworker showed us pictures and bios of four prospective couples.

The moment I read the third bio, I knew they were the ones. They were both teachers, and they'd already adopted a little boy.

"Maybe my baby won't feel so different with a brother who was also adopted," I said. As my mom and I were leaving, the caseworker accidentally let slip their name, "Steele," so I always knew at least that much about the baby girl I called Natalie Rose.

"I'll always love you," I whispered the day the social worker took her away, and every night I prayed that God would give my baby all the happiness life could offer.

My mom and dad split up when I was four, but my brother, Regan, and I always knew they loved us. After all, they'd picked us out special. But there was a part of me that never stopped wondering about my birth parents. Where did they live? What did they look like? Did I have any brothers or sisters?

Everywhere I went I studied total strangers, wondering if they could be the ones. "What if I met them somewhere and didn't even know it?" I asked my mom. On my sixteenth birthday she gave me a letter the social worker had passed along when she carried me home from the hospital.

"We brought you into this world out of love. Please keep me in your heart," I read, my eyes brimming with tears.

"I bet she's thinking about you this very minute," Mom said.

Every year on her birthday, I bought roses for my Natalie Rose and cried listening to Joni Mitchell sing about the baby she'd given up for adoption.

It broke my heart whenever I went to the mall and saw moms and daughters shopping together. Fred and I broke up before the baby was born and never saw one another again. I later married a different man and had a wonderful son named Christopher. But Natalie Rose was never out of my thoughts.

When Christopher was twelve, I told him he had a half-sister somewhere. "Can we go find her?" he asked, excitedly.

But I said no. "We have to wait till she's ready and hope she wants to find us," I explained, knowing there was a chance my daughter might hate me for what I'd done and never want anything to do with me.

My sister Dawn was also eager to find the niece she'd never known. "You have to register with the agency so if she wants to find you she can," she insisted. But Dawn did more than just rally me on—she became the instrument God used to fill the gaping hole in my heart.

After I graduated from high school, I moved from Burns Lake—a small northern British Columbia town—to North Vancouver to live with my dad and try to break into movie production work. I carried that application in my purse. I had it with me when I went to my job at the costume shop, visited friends or swam at the rec center pool with Dad and my half-siblings, Brendan and Michaela, from his second marriage.

And then one day Dad went swimming alone, and when he came home he pounded on my bedroom door. "Tara! Come quick! I have something incredible to tell you!"

Dawn works at the rec center, and she always noticed Charles Steele because she knew that was the surname of my baby's adoptive parents. "He has a son and a daughter, but she's too young," she told me once, but then one day Charles brought another daughter with him . . . and Dawn took one look at her and knew.

"She's just the right age, and I'd recognize those strong hands anywhere," my sister called to tell me. "They're your hands, Theresa. I think I found your daughter."

"No, it's too incredible," I said, refusing to get my hopes up only to have them dashed.

Dawn waited until a day when Charles came alone to the rec center, then cautiously asked, "By chance, do you have an adopted daughter?"

"Yes, her name is Tara," Charles replied, and when he said her birthday was October first, Dawn knew for sure.

I hugged my dad, then grabbed the phone to call my mom. "I found my birth mom!" I sobbed in near hysterics. Mom was thrilled for me because she already knew something I was just now learning for myself—that there was a giant piece of me that had been missing all my life. I hadn't kept that application in my purse so long because I was nervous about meeting my birth mom. I'd kept it because I was terrified it might not help and then I'd never, ever find her.

Dawn arranged for Tara to call me, and as I paced the floor I didn't know what to expect. A lifetime of questions were about to be answered, and I felt overwhelmed with joy, wonder and worry.

I'm not ready for this, I panicked, and just then the phone rang.

I don't even remember what Theresa and I talked about that first night. All I remember is the sound of her voice. "It's the voice that's been ringing inside my head my whole life," I told my mom later. "She's everything I always imagined."

Tara has my eyes and her father's nose. "You're beautiful," I sighed the day we met and fell into one another's arms. And later when I met Charles and Sharon, Tara's mom and dad, I knew I'd made the right decision all those years ago. "You've given her the life I never could have and raised a beautiful daughter," I said.

I tracked down Fred and told him about Dawn's miracle. He told me he'd been looking for her on the Internet, and when Sharon met Tara's birth dad she touched his chin and laughed, "Now I know where she got her dimples."

Theresa lives about an hour and a half from North Vancouver, and every time we get together we learn about even more things we share in common. We walk alike and gesture alike. We both love camping and swimming and bike-riding.

I loved meeting all my new uncles and aunts, my half-brother Christopher and my cousins. I couldn't wait for my twenty-second birthday when we threw a big party and everybody was there.

"I finally get to give you these in person," Theresa wept, handing me a big bouquet of roses.

Natalie Rose. I think it's such a beautiful name. Maybe one day, if I have a daughter of my own, that's what I'll name her, too.

Tara Steele
As told to Heather Black

10

THY WILL BE DONE

Thy kingdom come. Thy will be done on Earth, as it is in heaven.

Matthew 6:10

How Sweet the Sound

Take a harp, go about the city; make sweet melody, sing many songs, that thou may be remembered.

Isaiah 23:16

The lead should have been mine. All my friends agreed with me. At least, it shouldn't have been Helen's, that strange new girl. She never had a word to say, always looking down at her feet as if her life was too heavy to bear. We thought she was just stuck-up. *Things can't be all that bad for her,* we reasoned, *not with all the great clothes she wears.* She hadn't worn the same thing more than twice in the two months she'd been at our school.

But the worst of it was when she showed up at our tryouts and sang for my part. Everyone knew the lead role was meant for me. After all, I had parts in all our high-school musicals, and this was our senior year.

My friends were waiting for me, so I didn't hang around for Helen's audition. The shock came two days later when we hurried to check the bulletin board for the cast list.

We scanned the sheets looking for my name. When we found it, I stood there in shock. Helen was picked to play the lead! I was to be her mother and her understudy. Understudy? Nobody could believe it.

Rehearsals seemed to go on forever. Helen didn't seem to notice that we were going out of our way to ignore her. I'll admit it, Helen did have a beautiful voice. She was different on stage somehow. Not so much happy as settled and content.

Opening night brought its fair share of jitters. Everyone was quietly bustling around backstage, waiting for the curtain to go up. Everyone but Helen, of course. She seemed contained in her own world

The performance was a hit. Our timing was perfect; our voices blended and soared. Helen and I flowed back and forth, weaving the story between us—I, the ailing mother praying for her wayward daughter, and Helen, the daughter who realizes as her mother dies that there is more to life than this life. The final scene reached its dramatic end. I was laying in the darkened bedroom. The prop bed I was on was uncomfortable, which made it hard to stay still. I was impatient, anxious for Helen's big finish to be over.

She was spotlighted on stage, the grieving daughter beginning to understand the true meaning of the hymn she had been singing as her mother passed away.

"Amazing grace, how sweet the sound. . . ." Her voice lifted over the pain of her mother's death and the joy of God's promises.

". . . That saved a wretch like me . . ." Something real was happening to me as Helen sang. My impatience was gone.

". . . I once was lost, but now I'm found . . ." I started to cry.

". . . Was blind but now I see." My spirit began to turn within me, and I turned to God. In that moment, I knew his love, his desire for me. Helen's voice lingered in the prayer of the last note. The curtain dropped.

Complete silence. Not a sound. Helen stood behind the closed curtain, head bowed, gently weeping.

Suddenly, applause and cheers erupted, and when the curtain parted the entire audience was standing.

We all made our final bows. My hugs were genuine. My heart had been opened wide.

Then it was over. The costumes were hung up, makeup tissued off and the lights dimmed. Everyone went off in their usual groupings, congratulating each other.

Everyone but Helen. I stayed because I needed to tell her something.

"Helen, your song . . . it was so real for me," I hesitated, my feelings intense. I suddenly felt shy. "You sang me into the heart of God."

Helen's eyes met mine.

"That's what my mother said to me the night she died." A tear slipped down her cheek. My heart leapt to hers. "My mother was in such pain. Singing 'Amazing Grace' always comforted her. She told me to remember God would always be good to me, and that his grace would lead her home."

Her face lit up from the inside out, her mother's love shining through. "Just before she died, she whispered, 'Sing me into the heart of God, Helen.' That night and tonight, I sang for my mother."

Cynthia M. Hamond

The Final Cut

God brings men into deep waters not to drown them, but to cleanse them.

John H. Aughey

One swift movement of the razor, and I am on my way. No more racing thoughts, no more screams of anger—just fresh cuts, vibrant blood and a familiar euphoria. The blood creeps from the thin slices I have created, and soon comfort will be restored and sanity found. Another cut means more blood, but less pain. I examine my arm carefully—the cuts are not deep enough and the pain not strong enough. I must be careful, though; the marks might be noticed. I choose a different spot—my stomach. I quickly untuck the blouse of my uniform and tighten my abdomen.

I am sitting in my car and have only thirty minutes before school starts. The fight with my mom this morning is now a distant memory as I quickly bandage my latest wounds. Arriving at school, I quickly check to make sure nothing is showing. I open the car door, and it is like a whole new world, a world where nobody, not even my close friends, knows me well enough to notice the quiver of my lip or the unsteadiness of my hands. It is a world I play like a game, leaving emotions for the poets and drama for the actors. The morning air is crisp enough that my shallow breath can be seen as I make my way toward the entrance. People shout to say hello from all the corners of the parking lot as I wave and smile effortlessly. I mumble quietly to myself, *Let the games begin.*

I began hurting myself a long time ago. I can remember locking myself in the bathroom after a difficult day of elementary school or a fight with my parents and crying to God, asking Him for help, looking for someone or something to balm my pain. When no relief came, I would scratch my face, my arms, my legs—anything. Later, in middle school, my family went through the realization that country clubs and parochial schools cannot hide their children from the world of drugs. Watching from the sidelines as my oldest brother hit rock bottom and left for drug rehab, I made it my mission to hide every deep emotion I felt and started cutting each time these feelings crept into my conscience. I began using knives, razors and scissors— whatever would make me bleed. The blood made me stop hurting emotionally and start hurting physically. For me, dealing with the physical pain was nickels and dimes compared to some of the intense emotional pain I confronted in those first years of adolescence.

I could bandage my cuts and stop the bleeding, but I could never end my internal struggle with feeling valued by others unless I constantly appeared to be perfectly "normal." This meant hiding my problems, building those walls the therapists preach about and acting entirely unscathed by the turmoil I faced at home, in school, from my friends, from guys and from demanding athletic coaches. I became good at playing the part of the Patti

Mason everyone wanted to be around, rather than the Patti Mason I really was.

I would never have broken out from my cutting routine if it hadn't been for the presence of my faith in Jesus Christ. Soon, the cuts became too deep and scars set in, which led to questions and, finally, my confession. And as I slowly let the walls crumble, revealing the true me to my friends and family, I opened myself up to God for healing and protection. Now tears were the way my sadness was expressed.

Each day I got better. I discovered my faith again—my faith in life, in love, in myself and, above all, in Christ. It was through this faith that I realized the battle I was fighting would not end until I surrendered it to God and allowed myself to end the act. I had to feel the things inside, and I had to let people love the real me. I saw a therapist and was put on medication, and these two things definitely helped me to feel better. But getting myself back only happened when I surrendered to God. Resisting the urge to hurt myself is not something I could ever do by myself. God, and God alone, holds that power.

Patricia H. Mason

Believe in Me

It's hard to say that you're okay,
In the midst of hurt and strife.
You seek and find and persevere,
Through every stage of life.

You wonder what the future holds,
How successful you will be.
But you often fail to tell yourself,
"I believe in me."

You seek to find acceptance,
You conform to their new ways.
You lose hold of all your values,
And slowly drift astray.

Your passion soon becomes,
Something very hard to see.
Again you fail to tell yourself,
"I believe in me."

You search for joy and happiness,
But somehow come up short.
You didn't seek God's will this time,
Or wait for his report.

He wanted you to ask him,
"What is it that I need?"
So simple was the answer,
"Just believe in me."

Amy Alamillo

Finding My Eternal Summer

The summer after seventh grade, my best friend Richelle and I went to summer camp. The camp we chose was a Christian camp, but we chose it because it had water skiing and sailing!

After camp, I stayed with Richelle's family. Richelle's mom is my godmother, and I always feel at home when I stay with them. One night, I was cooking dinner with her mom, and out of the blue she asked me, "Katie, do you believe in God?" I didn't know what to say. I wasn't raised in a Christian family, and nobody had ever asked me that before.

"Yeah, I guess so," I told her.

"That means you're a Christian," she said, and she went on making dinner. I thought about the awkwardness of it all for a minute, and then just carried on.

The next year my life started going downhill. My parents were fighting all the time, and I was depressed and lonely. I began getting awful, debilitating headaches that would keep me in bed for weeks at a time. I ended up going in and out of the hospital while different doctors tried to figure out what was wrong with me. My grades were dropping, and my friends stopped calling me because I was hardly ever around. As summer was approaching, I began to get relief from the constant headaches. By June, I was well enough to go to camp. Once again, Richelle and I chose the Christian camp.

For some reason, I found the stability I had been missing in everyday life at camp. I felt safer with my fellow campers and our leaders than I did at home with my family. That summer I decided I wanted to be a Christian. Making this decision made me feel stronger.

I went home after camp hoping my life would be different than it had been the year before. I had a positive outlook on my future for the first time in a long while. But after a few weeks, the positive outlook was gone.

It was my first year of high school, and I was anxious about everything. I wanted so much to have the social life that I missed the prior year due to being sick. None of my friends were Christian, and when you're a teenager, being different doesn't work in your favor. I wanted so badly to have friends and to be included that I began to lie about who I was. I pretended to be "older" and said I had lots of experience with drugs and alcohol. To prove it, I started drinking and getting high.

At home, things were getting worse. My parents were still fighting, and there was no trust left in their relationship. My dad was never home, and my mom cried all the time. I became very depressed, and once again I was in and out of the hospital. As summer approached, my parents decided it was time to split up. And as I had every summer before, I went to camp. It was so incredible. When I got there, once again, all I wanted was to be "Christian."

Tenth grade is kind of a blur for me. I got back to school and started getting high again. I justified my drug use by telling myself that at least I wasn't doing any "heavy drugs" and that my drug use was minimal compared to most people's, but I ended up feeling just as guilty anyway. I tried going to church, but then I was ridiculed by my friends and family. I couldn't do anything right.

I had no internal peace. I tried to kill myself four times throughout the tenth grade, and my family had no idea. My parents got back together but split up again right before the summer. They were too preoccupied with their relationship problems to notice what I was going through. But no matter how much pain I was in, I was incapable of asking for help. I felt so alone. There were times when I didn't see the point of living anymore.

The next summer, I went to camp with a different attitude. This time, I didn't want to repeat the same scenario. I knew I could have a blast at camp by simply being there, but I wanted to be able to take that feeling home with me this time. I was ready to do the hardest thing for me to do—ask for help. I reached out first to my camp leader and told her I was scared to go home. I told her I was afraid I would hurt myself again. She held me and told me I didn't need to worry. God would always be with me. I knew she was right. I just wasn't able to see that before.

Now I'm sixteen and in eleventh grade. I am at a new school with new friends, a lot of whom go to my church. There are times when I am with friends who are Christians, and there are times when I'm with friends who aren't. My faith is now inside me. It's a personal choice, and I no longer need to be like everyone else. I'm how I want to be, and I know I am never alone.

Katie L. Schaan

As We Forgive Those

*F*orgive us our trespasses, as we forgive those
who trespass against us.

Matthew 6:12

"I cannot believe *she's* here!" I moaned to Brooke, my
friend and roommate. I had decided to go on the retreat to
get away from all the stress in my life, and I was ecstatic
when I discovered that my boyfriend, Mike, and Brooke
were also going. My excitement turned to dismay when I
discovered that the girl who was constantly trying to steal
my boyfriend was also going on the retreat. "Just look at
her! We haven't even left yet and she's already all over
him! Maybe this retreat wasn't such a good idea after all,"
I whined.

Brooke and I watched as Mike untangled himself from
Rachel and headed our way. "It's a test, Mol," Brooke
began. "It's a test from God. Are you up to it?"

"Hope so," I replied, as we piled into the car.

Once we arrived at the lodge, our team leaders did some
icebreakers to help us get to know each other. The first

icebreaker paired two people together. Guess who got paired together? Mike and Rachel. I glared as she snuggled up to Mike and asked him to tell her about himself. I looked over at Brooke, who was looking at me and mouthing the words, "Test from God."

It was time for a break, so I headed to the bathroom. I heard someone come in, then a voice said, "Well, she's his girlfriend now, but don't worry, because by the end of the retreat . . ." I stepped out of the stall, and sure enough it was Rachel talking to her friend. When she saw me she stopped talking and made a face that said, "Whatcha gonna do about it?" I returned her look with a glare and stormed out of the restroom in search of Brooke. When I told her what had happened, she replied just as she had earlier, "It's a test, Mol. I know you can handle this."

I didn't get the chance to respond because we were being corralled into small groups for discussion. Sure enough, when I arrived at the place where my group was to meet, she was the first person I saw. I could not believe my luck. I kept trying to think of what horrible thing I had done to make God punish me like this. Mike and I were finally together after a year and a half of struggling over whether or not to take our very close friendship to the next level. I didn't want to go through all of that again. I decided later that night I would talk to him. He wasn't showing any interest in her, but the fact that she was always next to him wherever he went was getting to me.

My thoughts were interrupted because small group discussion began. The topic was faith and spirituality, and everyone was sharing a little about his or her faith. When it was her turn, I listened to her talk about how she had lost members of her family this year and was very frustrated with God. "I don't really have any spirituality," she said, while staring at the floor.

During reflection time, her comment about not really

having any spirituality was all I could think about. *Did she really mean that?* I watched her sitting quietly across the room and knew she needed someone to talk to. Even though I had some extremely hostile feelings toward her, I knew she needed someone to reach out to her. I took a scrap of notebook paper and scribbled the following note: "I'm glad you're here this weekend! If you need someone to talk to, I'm willing to listen. God bless, Molly."

The next morning at breakfast, Rachel approached me. It wasn't until she got close that I realized she had tears in her eyes. "Thank you so much for your note," she told me. "You are the sweetest person!" She threw her arms around me and sobbed. I hugged her back for a very long time. When I looked up, Brooke was smiling at me from across the room.

That night, Mike and I went for a walk to talk about the situation. I explained to him what she said in the small group and told him about the note I had written to her. I wanted to be able to help her, but I didn't know if I could do it. I didn't even know if she wanted my help. After a while, we stopped and silently watched delicate snowflakes cover the ground in the season's first snow.

Mike made me feel better. "First of all, realize that nothing she can do will ever pull us apart. You and I are solid. I would never let that happen," he said. "And as for helping her, Molly, I know you can do it. Just be willing and then just let go and let God take care of the rest."

Mike was right. Once I let go and stopped "trying" to help her or "trying" to do the right thing, everything just fell into place. Rachel and I talked and shared our heartbreaks and our happiness. We learned a lot about each other. At times, she reminded me a little bit of myself.

As we prepared to leave the retreat, everyone was trying to say one last good-bye to the people they had shared so much with. When she and I found each other, we burst into tears and embraced. We stood there hugging each other as the group began to say the "Our Father" prayer. When they got to the part where it says, "Forgive us our trespasses as we forgive those who trespass against us," I realized I had figured out what that meant.

Before the retreat, I had been trying to deal with so many things—my mother had been seriously ill for months, I had two thesis papers due within the next two weeks, and I had gotten run down from trying to deal with it all. I felt like I was at the end of my rope. During the "Our Father," I realized that I had been given an opportunity to learn about the words in the prayer I had said so many times. All of the things I was so worried about before the retreat didn't seem so difficult anymore. I wasn't all alone.

Mike had been watching from across the room. I dried my eyes and walked to his open arms. "I love you," I said, smiling up at him.

He kissed me on the forehead and hugged me tight. "I just watched you grow," he said. I hugged him back. As we left camp I felt totally relaxed and happy. "Thy will be done" were now words I truly understood.

Molly Schumacher

Who Is Jack Canfield?

Jack Canfield is one of America's leading experts in the development of human potential and personal effectiveness. He is both a dynamic, entertaining speaker and a highly sought-after trainer. Jack has a wonderful ability to inform and inspire audiences toward increased levels of self-esteem and peak performance.

He is the author and narrator of several bestselling audio- and videocassette programs, including *The Success Principles, Self-Esteem and Peak Performance, How to Build High Self-Esteem, Self-Esteem in the Classroom* and *Chicken Soup for the Soul—Live.* He is regularly seen on television shows such as *Good Morning America, 20/20* and *NBC Nightly News.* Jack has coauthored numerous books, including the *Chicken Soup for the Soul* series, *Dare to Win* and *The Aladdin Factor* (all with Mark Victor Hansen), *100 Ways to Build Self-Concept in the Classroom* (with Harold C. Wells), *Heart at Work* (with Jacqueline Miller) and *The Power of Focus* (with Les Hewitt and Mark Victor Hansen).

Jack is a regularly featured speaker for professional associations, school districts, government agencies, churches, hospitals, sales organizations and corporations. His clients have included the American Dental Association, the American Management Association, AT&T, Campbell's Soup, Clairol, Domino's Pizza, GE, ITT, Hartford Insurance, Johnson & Johnson, the Million Dollar Roundtable, NCR, New England Telephone, Re/Max, Scott Paper, TRW and Virgin Records.

Jack conducts an annual eight-day Training of Trainers program in the areas of self-esteem and peak performance. It attracts educators, counselors, parenting trainers, corporate trainers, professional speakers, ministers and others interested in developing their speaking and seminar-leading skills.

For further information about Jack's books, tapes and training programs, or to schedule him for a presentation, please contact:

Self-Esteem Seminars
P.O. Box 30880
Santa Barbara, CA 93130
phone: 805-563-2935 • fax: 805-563-2945
Web site: *www.chickensoupforthesoul.com*

Who Is Mark Victor Hansen?

In the area of human potential, no one is better known and more respected than Mark Victor Hansen. For more than thirty years, Mark has focused solely on helping people from all walks of life reshape their personal vision of what's possible. His powerful messages of possibility, opportunity and action have helped create startling and powerful change in thousands of organizations and millions of individuals worldwide.

He is a sought-after keynote speaker, bestselling author and marketing maven. Mark's credentials include a lifetime of entrepreneurial success, in addition to an extensive academic background. He is a prolific writer with many bestselling books such as *The One Minute Millionaire, The Power of Focus, The Aladdin Factor* and *Dare to Win,* in addition to the *Chicken Soup for the Soul* series. Mark has also made a profound influence through his extensive library of audio programs, video programs and enriching articles in the areas of big thinking, sales achievement, wealth building, publishing success, and personal and professional development.

Mark is also the founder of MEGA Book Marketing University and Building Your MEGA Speaking Empire. Both are annual conferences where Mark coaches and teaches new and aspiring authors, speakers and experts on building lucrative publishing and speaking careers.

His energy and exuberance travel still further through mediums such as television (*Oprah,* CNN and *The Today Show*), print (*Time, U.S. News & World Report, USA Today, New York Times* and *Entrepreneur*) and countless radio and newspaper interviews as he assures our planet's people that *"you can easily create the life you deserve."*

As a passionate philanthropist and humanitarian, he's been the recipient of numerous awards that honor his entrepreneurial spirit, philanthropic heart and business acumen, including the prestigious Horatio Alger Award for his extraordinary life achievements, which stand as a powerful example that the free enterprise system still offers opportunity to all.

Mark Victor Hansen is an enthusiastic crusader of what's possible and is *driven* to make the world a better place.

Mark Victor Hansen & Associates, Inc.
P.O. Box 7665 • Newport Beach, CA 92658
phone: 949-764-2640 • fax: 949-722-6912
FREE resources online at: *www.markvictorhansen.com*

Who Is Kimberly Kirberger?

Kim Kirberger is one of the most renowned and effective champions for teens today. Deeply committed to improving the often-torturous transition from adolescence to adulthood, Kim's books, public speaking, advice columns and teen-help organizations make it safer for teens to love and accept who they are. In the compassionate and loving voice that teens all over the world turn to and trust, Kim reassures the frightened, guides the confused, and incites hope where often too little exists.

Kim's astonishing ability to capture the teen voice propelled her onto the #1 *New York Times* bestseller slot on more than one occasion, first as coauthor of *Chicken Soup for the Teenage Soul,* which catapulted her to international recognition. Kim's success inspired an outpouring of thousands of candid letters and intimate submissions from teens around the globe, which set the stage for *Chicken Soup for the Teenage Soul II* and *III,* both debuting at the #1 spot on the *New York Times* bestseller list. Her other releases in the *Chicken Soup* family include *Chicken Soup for the Teenage Soul Journal, Chicken Soup for the Parent's Soul, Chicken Soup for the College Soul, Chicken Soup for the Teenage Soul on Tough Stuff* and *Chicken Soup for the Teenage Soul on Love & Friendship.* Kim went on to create the *Teen Love* series, the first of which, a *New York Times* bestseller, has sold more than 700,000 books since its publication in 1999. Kim's latest project is *No Body's Perfect: Stories by Teens About Body Image, Self-Acceptance and the Search for Identity. No Body's Perfect* and the accompanying *No Body's Perfect Journal* were released by Scholastic in January 2003.

Kim's lecture schedule includes nonprofit organizations, corporate groups and high schools. Kim's television appearances include *Geraldo,* MSNBC, Fox Family's *Parenting 101,* CNN, CBS's *Woman to Woman* and *The Terry Bradshaw Show.* She has written a cover story on "Teenagers Today" for *Life* magazine, as well as consulted and written for *Teen, Seventeen, Cosmo Girl, Teen People, Twist, J-14* and *Jump.*

Kim grew up attending a Baptist church in the small town of Clarksburg, West Virginia. In keeping with her steadfast dedication to her religion, she sent her weekly allowance to Billy Graham. It is her prayer that, through this book and its stories of faith and love, teens will find their way to God from whom all blessings flow. Kim lives in Southern California with her teenage son, Jesse.

Who Is Patty Aubery?

Patty Aubery is the president of Chicken Soup for the Soul Enterprises, Inc. Patty has been working with Jack and Mark since the birth of *Chicken Soup for the Soul.*

Patty is the coauthor of *Chicken Soup for the Surviving Soul, Chicken Soup for the Christian Soul, Chicken Soup for the Expectant Mother's Soul, Chicken Soup for the Christian Family Soul, Chicken Soup for the Christian Woman's Soul* and *Chicken Soup for the Sister's Soul.* She has been a guest on over 150 local and nationally syndicated radio shows.

Patty is married to Jeff Aubery, and together they have two wonderful children, J. T. and Chandler. Patty and her family reside in Santa Barbara, California, and she can be reached at:

Self-Esteem Seminars, Inc.
P.O. Box 30880
Santa Barbara, CA 93130
phone: 805-563-2935
fax: 805-563-2945

Who Is Nancy Mitchell-Autio?

Nancy Mitchell-Autio is the Director of Story Acquisitions for the *Chicken Soup for the Soul* series. She graduated from Arizona State University in May 1994 with a B.S. in Nursing. After graduation, Nancy worked at Good Samaritan Regional Medical Center in Phoenix, Arizona, in the Cardiovascular Intensive Care Unit. In September 1994, Nancy moved back to her native Los Angeles and became involved with the *Chicken Soup* series. Nancy's intentions were to help finish *A 2nd Helping of Chicken Soup for the Soul* and then return to nursing. However, in December of that year, she was asked to continue on full-time as part of the *Chicken Soup* team. Nancy put nursing on hold and became Director of Story Acquisitions, working closely with Jack and Mark on all *Chicken Soup for the Soul* projects.

Nancy says that what she is most thankful for is her move back to L.A., where she could be there for her mother, Linda Mitchell, during her bout with breast cancer. Out of that struggle, Nancy coauthored, along with her sister, Patty Aubery, *Chicken Soup for the Surviving Soul: 101 Stories of Courage and Inspiration from Those Who Have Survived Cancer.* Little did she know that the book would become her own inspiration when her dad was diagnosed with prostate cancer in 1999.

Nancy also coauthored *Chicken Soup for the Christian Soul, Chicken Soup for the Christian Family Soul, Chicken Soup for the Expectant Mother's Soul, Chicken Soup for the Nurse's Soul* and *Chicken Soup for the Sister's Soul.* Nancy resides in Santa Barbara with her husband, Kirk Autio, daughter, Molly Anne, and dogs Kona, Floyd and Cora.

You may contact Nancy Mitchell-Autio at:

Self-Esteem Seminars, Inc.
P.O. Box 30880
Santa Barbara, CA 93130
phone: 805-682-6311
fax: 805-682-0872
e-mail: *nautio@chickensoupforthesoul.com*

Contributors

Kristina J. Adams received her Bachelor of Science in Education from Indiana Wesleyan University in 1995. She is currently teaching exploratory Spanish and German at the middle-school level in Middlebury, Indiana, and working toward her master's degree. She lives with her husband, Ryan, a police officer, and daughter, Mackenzie.

Amy Alamillo is a student at the University of Central Florida. She loves to read and write, and her favorite sport is baseball. Amy hopes to establish a career in psychology or journalism. Please e-mail her at *Faith 513@aol.com.*

Michael Ambrosio was forever captured by the spirit of faith and adventure through his many years of surfing, complete with exhilarating wave rides and near-death experiences. He writes stories for children and teens, and lives with his wife and five children in Folsom, California. For more information, visit *www.lionxpublishing.com.*

Marsha Arons is a freelance writer and video producer. Her stories and articles have appeared in *Good Housekeeping, Reader's Digest, Redbook, Woman's Day* and *Woman's World.* She has contributed to eleven of the books in the *Chicken Soup for the Soul* book series. She is married and the mother of four daughters.

Heather Black is a frequent contributor to *Woman's World Magazine.*

Marion Blanchard is a published freelance writer/poet. She writes about her life experience. She maintains that without prayers and faith, all the trials and suffering in life would destroy us. Marion is a firm believer in sharing what has helped us to heal. "We must pass on to others in hopes that it will also help them on this journey we call life."

Abby Danielle Burlbaugh is currently attending Harding University in pursuit of her Bachelor of Arts in English Literature. She writes mainly short stories and poetry. She enjoys reading, writing, crocheting and cooking. Abby plans to travel to Ireland with her husband and write for a living.

Amy Rene Byrne is a seventeen-year-old from Cookeville, Tennessee.

She plays volleyball and runs track, is a member of the CHS Speech Team and participates in other drama productions. She is an active member of Interact, Beta, Mu Alpha Theta, FCA, Culture Awareness Club, and Film Club. E-mail Amy at *amybyrne@hotmail.com.*

Trish E. Calvarese is a high-school sophomore in Littleton, Colorado. She plays volleyball, basketball, soccer and enjoys skiing. She is an editor of her school newspaper, an orator on her school's speech and debate team, and a member of Big Brothers Big Sisters of America.

Michele Wallace Campanelli is a national bestselling author. She writes short stories and has penned several novels, including *Keeper of the Shroud* and *Margarita,* published by Americana Books. Her personal editor is Fontaine M. Wallace. To contact Michele, go to *www. michelecampanelli.com.*

Allison Carlyon is currently a high-school senior. Next year she plans to attend St. Norberts College. She enjoys playing guitar, running, skiing, attending various Christian youth activities, and spending time with friends and family. Please e-mail her at *alli_c@hotmail.com.*

Anastasia Cassidy is a high-school junior (class of 2005) in Michigan. She enjoys eating bacon, sleeping late, correcting improper grammar and collecting merchandise that features a duck motif. She dislikes the color mauve, clowns and chores involving litter boxes and/or used dishes. Some people don't understand her humor.

Tim Chaney is a graduate of the University of Colorado–Boulder. He is currently a U.S. Peace Corps volunteer teaching science and health education in Kenya with his wife Sarah. After returning to America, he hopes to purse a M.A. in secondary education. Please reach him at *tjc4@georgetown.edu.*

Hugh T. Chapman, a former special-education teacher, now teaches high-school business classes in Brockwell, Arkansas. Hugh, his wife Julie, son Dustin and daughter Danielle make their home in Horseshoe Bend, Arkansas. He remains in close contact with Jason's grandparents and would love to hear from you. You may e-mail Hugh at *Julchapman@yahoo.com.*

Lana L. Comstock has been a Christian since 1984. She has one daughter who she has homeschooled for eleven years. Her hobbies are natural health studies and writing. Lana teaches history classes and does bookkeeping part-time. She has been married for sixteen very happy years. Contact her at *healthesteem@aol.com*.

Cheryl Costello-Forshey's poetry has been published in numerous *Chicken Soup* books as well as *Stories for a Teen's Heart, Stories for a Faithful Heart, Stories for a Teen's Heart 2, A Pleasant Place* and *Serenity for a Woman's Heart*. Cheryl can be reached at *costello-forshey@1st.net*.

Bethany Couts will graduate from Ohio University in June 2004. She will then serve in the Peace Corps. Upon returning, she will look for a job in the sport industry. She is a youth leader who enjoys photography, hockey, traveling and missions work/community service. Please reach her at *bc124900@ohiou.edu*.

Kelli Czarnick received her Bachelor of Science in Human and Social Service Administration from Bellevue University in 2002. She plans on becoming a Licensed Mental Health Practitioner after receiving her Master of Science in Counseling. She enjoys traveling, reading and working with people. She can be reached at *Kelli5679@charter.net*.

Jenny DeYaeger is a sixteen-year-old junior in high school. She lives with her mom, dad and sister in Rochester, New York. She plans to graduate in 2004 and major in elementary education. Her main goal in life is to make a difference wherever and whenever she can.

Christina Marie Dotson is majoring in elementary education at Ashland University. She lives in Ohio with her wonderful mother and two awesome younger brothers. Christina enjoys Rollerblading, nature photography and yard work. She dreams of writing children's books and making a difference in kids' lives. She can be reached at *chrissyd@accnorwalk.com*.

Gary Flaherty is a born-again Christian and is currently writing a Christian fiction novel. He is an avid reader of Christian materials. He and his wife, Cindy, love the outdoors and spending time with youth. Please e-mail them at *GaryandCindy@mylifeline.net*.

Randy Glasbergen is one of America's most widely and frequently published cartoonists. More than 25,000 of his cartoons have been published by *Funny Times, Reader's Digest, Guideposts for Teens, Campus Life, Group Magazine* and many others. His daily comic panel, "The Better Half," is syndicated worldwide by King Features Syndicate. He is also the author of three cartooning instruction books and several cartoon anthologies. To read a cartoon a day, please visit Randy's Web site at *www.glasbergen.com.*

Kristy Glassen is a recent graduate of Penn State University in State College, Pennsylvania. She has previously been published in *Chicken Soup for the Teenage Soul on Tough Stuff* and *Chicken Soup for the Teenage Soul on Love and Friendship.* She was the grand-prize winner in the *Chicken Soup* "What's Your Definition of Love?" contest in 1999. She can be reached at *psukristy21@hotmail.com.*

Cynthia M. Hamond, S.F.O., began writing five years ago. Cynthia has been published in several *Chicken Soup for the Soul* and *Stories for the Heart* books, as well as in magazines, and has received two awards. Her story "Goodwill" (*Chicken Soup for the Kid's Soul*) was featured on the *Chicken Soup for the Soul* television series and Fox Kids. Contact Cynthia at *Candbh@aol.com.*

Jonny Hawkins is a full-time, freelance cartoonist from Sherwood, Michigan. Thousands of his cartoons have appeared in over 265 publications over the last seventeen years. His "Solomon Bear and Friends" can be found on a product line called "Scripture Teachers" at *LCPGifts.com.* His books with Bob Phillips—*Heavenly Humor* and *A Tackle Box of Fishing Funnies*—are available in bookstores or by contacting him at *jonnyhawkins2nz@yahoo.com.*

Christy Heitger-Casbon, a regular contributing writer to several Christian magazines, specializes in the teen market. She also writes frequently about women's issues as well as pet health and safety. Christy lives in Tallahassee, Florida, with her husband, Todd, and enjoys running and boating. Please e-mail her at *christy_heitger_casbon@hotmail.com.*

Adrianna Hutchinson loves to write and feels it's the most rewarding method of expressing herself. She believes she has an "alive" spirit that she spreads to those around her through writing. She receives wonderful support from friends who are her family, as well as her real family. She is extremely blessed with them all. E-mail her at *xxheavensangelxx@hotmail.com*.

Corinne Ingram attends Hannibal-LaGrange College, majoring in secondary English education. Corinne has enjoyed writing poetry and short stories since she was in junior high. She plans to graduate from Hannibal-LaGrange in May 2005, get married, and begin teaching and writing on the side.

Ben Jenkins is a high-school student in New Westminster British Columbia. He enjoys hanging out with his friends and having late-night discussions about life over a cup of coffee or tea. Ben spends a lot of time doing things related to self-exploration and also enjoys cliff jumping, skateboarding, playing music and talking to his family. Please e-mail him at *phoenixone@telus.net*.

Shelly Teems Johnson earned her associate degree in science from Gainesville College and is currently working on her bachelor's degree in physical education from Kennesaw State University. She enjoys camping, skiing, deer hunting, fishing, reading and spending time with her family. Shelly plans to teach high-school physical education in the future.

Julie Johnston is an eighteen-year-old dwarf, standing three feet tall. She's also visually impaired, and yet she's a straight-A student in high school. She loves to sing and has performed many times in retirement homes and church. She also enjoys speaking to younger kids and her peers about what it is like to be different and how to make the best of what life gives you. She's an accomplished writer, having won first place in the *Guideposts for Teens* essay contest in 1999. Her essay was entitled "Attitude Is Everything." Julie lives what she writes.

Brittany Lynn Jones is an honors student in high school. She's the sophomore class president, belongs to three clubs, and participates in cheerleading, volleyball and soccer. She's also very active in church and in two youth groups. She says she lives her life for James, who died at age thirteen.

Bil Keane created "The Family Circus" in 1960 and gathered most of his ideas from his only family: wife Thel and their five children. Now read by an estimated 188 million people daily, nine grandchildren provide much of the inspiration for the award-winning feature. Visit the Web site at *www.familycircus.com*.

Crystal Kirgiss lives in Minnesota with her husband and three teenaged sons. She is an author and speaker. In her spare time, she enjoys reading, volunteering for Young Life, and playing piano for the local high-school choirs and musical productions.

Jane Kise is the coauthor of *Did You Get What You Prayed For?* and *Find Your Fit: Dare to Act on God's Design for You.* Find out more about her books and consulting work with urban schools by visiting *www.janekise.com*.

Kerri Knipper is currently a freshman at William Paterson University. She is majoring in communications and hopes to one day work in television. She's always enjoyed writing, and this is her first publication. She wants to thank her family and friends for all their support. E-mail her at *HeavenzAngel584@aol.com*.

Erik Kreps graduated *cum laude* from Concordia University in 1994. He resides in Michigan with his wife and three children. Erik's cartoons have appeared in various Christian and secular publications, and he currently has several children's books in the works. He can be reached at *3grapes@email.com*.

Hallie Lantana received her M.F.A. in creative writing from Mills College in Oakland, California. She teaches creative writing in Madison, Wisconsin, and is currently working on a young-adult novel set in the Caribbean. Please e-mail her at *hallielantana@yahoo.com*.

April Linck has lived her whole life in Baytown, Texas. She is an aspiring author, and enjoys music and reading.

Patricia H. Mason moved to Colorado from Pennsylvania after graduating from high school. Currently she is pursuing a degree in journalism at Colorado State University. Patti enjoys outdoor activities and sports such as hiking, soccer, snowboarding and camping.

Walker Meade began to write stories at age fourteen. When he was twenty-two, one of his pieces was published in *Colliers* magazine. He then wrote short fiction for the *Saturday Evening Post, Good Housekeeping* and *Gentleman's Quarterly,* among others. Subsequently, he turned to writing nonfiction for magazines such as *Cosmopolitan, Reader's Digest* and *Redbook.* Later he became the managing editor of *Cosmopolitan* and then the managing editor of *Reader's Digest* Condensed Book Club. His last position in publishing was as president and editor-in-chief of Avon Books. Today he is retired and concentrating on writing longer fiction. Upstart Press published his first novel in August 2001. It has had exciting critical reception and is selling unusually well. The book, *Unspeakable Acts,* can be ordered from *Amazon.com.* He has just finished his second novel.

Andrea Mendez is a junior in high school, living in New York. In addition to writing, Andrea's passions include music and theater. She works back stage as well as on the stage, and hopes to continue both writing and performing in college.

Johanna Olson received her bachelor of arts degree, with honors, from Luther College in 2002. She is continuing to run competitively with the hopes of competing in the Olympic trials. Johanna enjoys running, skiing, swimming, spending time with family and working with children. She plans to become a collegiate distance running coach.

Mark Parisi's "Off the Mark" comic panel has been syndicated since 1987 and is distributed by United Media. Mark's humor also graces greeting cards, T-shirts, calendars, magazines (such as *Billboard*), newsletters and books. Lynn, his wife/business partner, and their daughter, Jenny, contribute inspiration (as do three cats).

Casey Glynn Patriarco is a sixteen-year-old sophomore in Allentown, Pennsylvania. She enjoys the creative arts, and expresses herself through creative writing, poetry and stage work. She also is exploring public speaking in school as well as the performing arts, including dance. She thanks her inspirational brother, Vincent, now seven years old.

Kristi Powers and her husband Michael have been involved in youth ministry for seventeen years. They authored the book *Heart Touchers,* and their stories appear in several inspirational books, including many in the *Chicken Soup* series. They invite you to join the thousands of readers on their inspirational e-mail list at *www.Heart4Teens.com*. E-mail Kristi at *NoodlesP29@aol.com*.

Michael T. Powers, whose writing appears in fourteen inspirational books, including many in the *Chicken Soup* series, is a motivational speaker, high-school girls' coach, founder of *Heart4Teens.com*, and has been involved in youth ministry for seventeen years. Preview his book, *Heart Touchers*, or join the thousands of worldwide readers on his inspirational e-mail list by visiting *www.HeartTouchers.com*. E-mail him at *Heart4Teens@aol.com*.

Nathan Roy is an eighth-grader at a private school in Oklahoma. He is very involved in sports at school, and especially enjoys football and baseball. Nathan plans on going to the University of Oklahoma to study medicine upon graduation from high school. Ultimately, Nathan desires God's direction for his life.

Katie L. Schaan graduated from high school in 2002 and is now looking forward to what God has planned for her future. She continues to go to camp, as part of the staff now rather than a camper, and is very involved with leading the youth ministries at her church.

Molly Schumacher works as a residence hall director at Loras College in Dubuque, Iowa. When she's not working with college students, Molly enjoys spending time with her husband, Mike, her nine-month-old son, Max, and dog, Shelby. Her future plans include furthering her career in college student affairs and further exploration of her passion for writing. She can be reached at *mburrows@loras.edu*.

Harley Schwadron's cartoons appear in many publications, including *Barron's*, *Wall Street Journal*, *Bulletin of the Atomic Scientists*, *Medical Economics* and *Harvard Business Review*. He worked as a newspaper reporter, editor, and university magazine and PR editor. He has been a full-time cartoonist since 1984. He can be reached at P.O. Box 1347, Ann Arbor, MI 48106, phone/fax: 734-426-8433.

Bethany Schwartz, a 2003 graduate of Houghton College, hopes to someday write Christian books for young adults. When not writing, she enjoys photography, graphic design, Macintosh computers, football and camping. You can e-mail her at *bee@babythunder.net* or visit her Web site at *www.babythunder.net.*

Jenny Sharaf is a currently a senior in high school and planning to attend Emerson College in the fall. She works for the *Chicken Soup for the Teenage Soul* series as a teen editor and contributing writer. Her work has been published in many *Chicken Soup* books, and she has a poem in the book *No Body's Perfect.*

Ashleigh Kittle Slater is a 2001 graduate of the University of Hawaii at Hilo and a current graduate student at Regent University. Her writing has been published in *Campus Life* and *Brio,* as well as on *www.allmusic.com.* Ashleigh and her husband, Ted, live in Virginia. Please contact her at *slater@ijot.com.*

Gloria Cassity Stargel has been published in *Guideposts, Decision* and other magazines. She authored *The Healing: One Family's Victorious Struggle with Cancer,* an award-winning book that will strengthen your faith. Read portions of the book or order it at *www.brightmorning.com.* You can also order by contacting Applied Images, 312 Bradford St., N.W., Gainesville, GA 30501, phone: 800-888-9529.

Mary Stedham is a licensed professional counselor whose practice is in Texas. A former schoolteacher, Mary also leads seminars and workshops, and enjoys an opportunity to encourage or inspire others with her words. You may contact her at *marystedham@cs.com.*

Becky Steinberg is eighteen years old and plans to attend Columbia College Chicago to receive a degree in writing. In the future, she plans to write many inspirational books and poetry. Her goal is to touch the souls of those who read her books and stories.

Whitney Thetford has always been very active, and her passion for singing and performing started when she was a child. After being sick, she decided nursing was to be her career. Her passion to perform is being fulfilled at The Nashville Follies Musical Theater in Nashville, Indiana, where she has performed every weekend since June 2002.

LeAnn Thieman is a nationally acclaimed speaker and author. A member of the National Speakers Association, LeAnn inspires audiences to balance their lives, truly live their priorities and make a difference in the world. She has written stories for nine *Chicken Soup* books and is coauthor of *Chicken Soup for the Nurse's Soul* and *Chicken Soup for the Christian Woman's Soul.* You can contact LeAnn at 6600 Thompson Drive, Fort Collins, CO 80526; *www.LeAnnThieman.com*; or call toll-free 1-877-THIEMAN.

Bernard "Richie" Thomassen graduated from high school in Nyack, New York, in 2003. He is currently an intern with Jacques Roc Productions. Richie enjoys performing in off-Broadway productions and standup comedy clubs, writing music, and playing guitar, piano, bassoon and trumpet. He plans to major in music production and technology. Please e-mail him at *RichieThomassen@aol.com.*

Sara Torina is currently a junior in high school and lives in Melrose Park, Illinois. She plans to major in English in college. She enjoys writing for her school newspaper, is a member of the National Honor Society and is on a dance team. You can reach Sara at *SaraT12385@aol.com.*

Mary Cornelia Van Sant, nicknamed Connie at birth, is a native South Carolinian. She's been an occupational therapist since 1979, currently working in the Arizona public schools. Connie rediscovered her passion for writing after moving to Arizona in 1989. Other published works thus far include articles for twelve-step recovery journals.

Melanie Walenciak is a writer and homeschooling mom who lives in Tulsa, Oklahoma. These days, she gets hugs from her true Romeo, Jim, and their precious sons, Cody and Dillon. And she still cherishes the hugs she gets from her daddy.

Joseph B. Walker began his professional writing career as a staff writer for the *Deseret News* in Salt Lake City, eventually becoming that newspaper's television and live theater critic. He has also done extensive work in public relations. Since 1990 he has written a weekly newspaper column called *ValueSpeak,* which has appeared in more than 200 newspapers nationally. His published books include *How Can You Mend a Broken Spleen? Home Remedies for an Ailing World* for Deseret Books, *The Mission: Inside the Church of Jesus Christ of Latter-Day Saints* for

Warner Books and four ghostwriting projects. Joseph and his wife, Anita, are parents of five children. They reside in American, Utah.

Meredith Wertz attends Penn State University. Her major is public relations, with a double minor in business and sociology. Meredith is a member of PRSSA, the National Honor Society, and the sorority Alpha Sigma Alpha. She enjoys vacationing at the beach and spending time with her family and friends.

Annie Wignall is the founder and director of Care Bags Foundation, a nonprofit organization she began in January 2000 that provides "Care Bags" to displaced, abused and disadvantaged children worldwide. Annie plans to be a teacher when she grows up. To help Annie and to learn more about Care Bags, please visit *www.carebags4kids.org.*

Lindsay Beth Wondero is studying to receive her Bachelor of Arts degree from Michigan State University, majoring in advertising with a specialization in public relations. Lindsay enjoys writing, traveling, camping, and playing volleyball and softball. She plans to continue her education after graduation. Please e-mail her at *wonderoL@msu.edu.*

Lynne Zielinski of Huntsville, Alabama, is a frequent contributor to *Chicken Soup for the Soul* books. A freelance writer and book reviewer, Lynne believes life is a gift from God and what we do with it is our gift to God. You can reach her at *arisway@aol.com.*

Permissions

Chicken Soup for the Soul®

Improving Your Life Every Day

Real people sharing real stories — for nineteen years. Now, Chicken Soup for the Soul has gone beyond the bookstore to become a world leader in life improvement. Through books, movies, DVDs, online resources and other partnerships, we bring hope, courage, inspiration and love to hundreds of millions of people around the world. Chicken Soup for the Soul's writers and readers belong to a one-of-a-kind global community, sharing advice, support, guidance, comfort, and knowledge.

Chicken Soup for the Soul stories have been translated into more than 40 languages and can be found in more than one hundred countries. Every day, millions of people experience a Chicken Soup for the Soul story in a book, magazine, newspaper or online. As we share our life experiences through these stories, we offer hope, comfort and inspiration to one another. The stories travel from person to person, and from country to country, helping to improve lives everywhere.

Share with Us

We all have had Chicken Soup for the Soul moments in our lives. If you would like to share your story or poem with millions of people around the world, go to chickensoup.com and click on "Submit Your Story." You may be able to help another reader, and become a published author at the same time. Some of our past contributors have launched writing and speaking careers from the publication of their stories in our books!

Our submission volume has been increasing steadily — the quality and quantity of your submissions has been fabulous. We only accept story submissions via our website. They are no longer accepted via mail or fax.

To contact us regarding other matters, please send us an e-mail through webmaster@chickensoupforthesoul.com, or fax or write us at:

Chicken Soup for the Soul
P.O. Box 700
Cos Cob, CT 06807-0700
Fax: 203-861-7194

One more note from your friends at Chicken Soup for the Soul: Occasionally, we receive an unsolicited book manuscript from one of our readers, and we would like to respectfully inform you that we do not accept unsolicited manuscripts and we must discard the ones that appear.

Chicken Soup for the Soul

for the Soul.

Our 101 BEST STORIES

CHRISTIAN Teen Talk

Christian Teens Share Their Stories of Support, Inspiration and Growing Up

Jack Canfield
& Mark Victor Hansen
edited by Amy Newmark

Devout Christian teens care about their connection and relationship with God, but they are also experiencing all the normal ups and downs of teenage life. This book provides support to teens who care about their faith and are navigating their teenage years. With 101 heartfelt, true stories from Chicken Soup for the Soul's library about love, compassion, loss, forgiveness, friends, school, faith, and tough issues too, such as substance abuse, teen pregnancy, and divorce.

978-1-935096-12-2

Chicken Soup for the Soul

for the Soul

Our 101 BEST STORIES

Teens Talk Tough Times

Stories about the Hardest Parts of Being a Teenager

Jack Canfield
& Mark Victor Hansen
edited by Amy Newmark

Being a teenager is difficult even under idyllic circumstances. But when bad things happen, the challenges of being a teenager can be overwhelming, leading to self-destructive behavior, eating disorders, substance abuse, and other challenges. In addition, many teens are faced with illness, car accidents, loss of loved ones, divorces, or other upheavals. These 101 stories from Chicken Soup for the Soul's library describe the toughest teenage challenges and how to overcome them.

978-1-935096-03-0

Chicken Soup for the Soul
for the Soul

Teens Talk
Growing Up

Our
101
BEST
STORIES

Stories about Growing Up,
Meeting Challenges, and
Learning from Life

Jack Canfield
& Mark Victor Hansen
edited by Amy Newmark

Being a teenager is hard—school is challenging, college
and career are looming on the horizon, family issues arise,
friends and love come and go, bodies and emotions go
through major changes, and many teens experience the
loss of a loved one for the first time. This book reminds
teenagers that they are not alone, as they read stories written by other teens about the problems and issues they all
face every day.

978-1-935096-01-6

Chicken Soup for the Soul.

Teens Talk Relationships

Our **101** BEST STORIES

Stories about Family, Friends and Love

Jack Canfield & Mark Victor Hansen

edited by Amy Newmark

The teenage years are difficult. Old friends drift away, new friends come with new issues, teens fall in and out of love, and relationships with family members change. This book reminds teenagers that they are not alone, as they read the 101 best stories from Chicken Soup for the Soul's library written by other teens just like themselves, about the problems and issues they face every day—stories about friends, family, love, loss, and many lessons learned.

978-1-935096-06-1

Teenage years are tough, but this book will help teens as they journey through the ups and downs of adolescence. Teens will find support and inspiration in the 101 new stories from teens just like them. Stories in this book serve as a guide on topics about daily pressures of life, school, love, friendships, parents, and much more. This collection will show readers that as tough as things can get, they are not alone!

978-1-935096-72-6

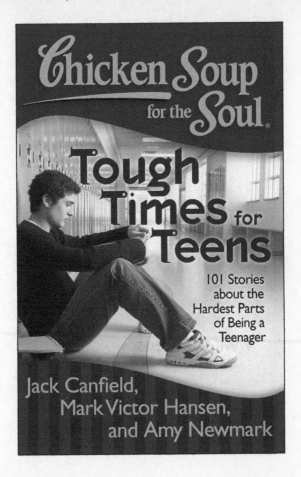

Chicken Soup for the Soul
for the Soul
Tough Times for Teens

101 Stories about the Hardest Parts of Being a Teenager

Jack Canfield,
Mark Victor Hansen,
and Amy Newmark

The teenage years are tough, and when bad things happen, the challenges can be overwhelming. Faced with illness, car accidents, loss of loved ones, divorces, or other upheavals, the obstacles to happiness can seem insurmountable. The 101 stories in this book describe the toughest teenage challenges and how other teens, with the same struggles, overcame them. This collection will be a support and companion for teenagers and will encourage, comfort, and inspire them, showing them that, as tough as things can get, they are not alone.

978-1-935096-80-1